Phonics Seatwork

Reproducible Worksheets for Phonics Practice

Marilyn Burch

MAKEMASTER® Blackline Masters

Fearon Teacher Aids
a division of
David S. Lake Publishers
Belmont, California

ISBN–0–8224–5543–9

Printed in the United States of America

1. 9 8 7 6 5 4 3

Table of Contents

Title	Sound	Page	Title	Sound	Page
Follow the Numbers	b	1	Find the Way	ay	33
Hard or Soft?	c	2	Coast Along	oa	34
Dollar Bank	d	3	Uptown and Downtown in My Town	ow	35
A Fancy Fan	f	4	Show Me a Rainbow	ow	36
Magic Drawing	g	5	What's He Shouting About?	ou	37
High on the Hill	h	6	What's Boiling?	oi	38
Fill the Jar!	j	7	Jump for Joy!	oy	39
Mystery Picture	k	8	Fill the Balloons	o͞o	40
Look and Learn	l	9	A New Kind of Stew	ew	41
Match the Mittens	m	10	The Autumn Leaves Are Falling	au	42
No, No, No!	n	11	I Saw These Claws	aw	43
Pick a Picture	p	12	The Garden	ar	44
Quilting Party	q	13	What Is It?	er	45
Rake the Leaves!	r	14	Secret Code	ir	46
Something Starts with S	s	15	A Corny Story	or	47
T Time!	t	16	A Surprise Picture for You	ur	48
A Twisting Vine	v	17	Search for the Cheese	ch	49
Wide and Wild Wings	w	18	Special Shoes	sh	50
The Box That Was X-Rayed	x	19	Think About This	th	51
A Page for the Y's	y	20	What Is This Picture?	wh	52
Zip the Zipper!	z	21	Mend the Breaks	br	53
A Day Behind the Gate	ā	22	The Crying Crocodile	cr	54
The Leaf Family	ē, e͞e, ēa	23	A Dry Dragon	dr	55
Help the Vines Grow	ī	24	Help the Frog and His Friend	fr	56
Fill in the Words	ō	25	Trace the Trail	tr	57
This Makes Music	ū	26	A Surprise Picture	fl	58
The Boy with the Cap	ă	27	Spin and Spell	sp	59
Ring the Bell	ĕ	28	A Picture Surprise	sk	60
Fill the Glass with Milk!	ĭ	29			
Follow the Dots!	ŏ	30			
A Puzzle for Fun	ŭ	31			
Stained Glass Window	ai	32			

To the Teacher

Phonics Seatwork is a completely reproducible collection of 60 seat assignments for phonics practice and reinforcement of basic phonics skills. The wide variety of activities includes:

- cut-and-paste projects
- magic pictures
- choosing words from lists to match picture clues
- using words from lists to write stories
- dot-to-dot pictures
- crossword puzzles

Many of these activities can be expanded, so that children can take them home and continue working on them, alone or with parental supervision.

Of course, you will have to read the directions aloud to the children. In some cases, you may have to supervise the children closely, especially when they are using scissors and glue. The writing assignments (pages 11, 12, 22, 23, 27, 28, 35, 36, and 43) and one crossword puzzle (page 51) are more difficult than some of the other pages. These should be done as group activities, with teacher supervision. The word lists have some words that are incorrect. Tell the children to choose only those that are correct.

Have the following materials available: crayons, paste, scissors, pencils, and construction paper. Occasionally, you will need other, easily obtainable supplies. These are listed on the individual pages.

Many of the finished projects can be displayed in the classroom. These activities coordinate well with any phonics program.

Follow the Numbers

On the lines, print words
that start with the same sound as  .
Starting with **1**, draw a line
from dot to dot.

•2

•3

1•   •4

9•   •10 •5   6•

8•   7•

Word List

bag   box   back   dog   bus   belt   doll   bat

ball   dig   baby   deer   but   bad   big   best

Hard or Soft?

Read the words. If the **c** sounds like an **s**, circle it. If the **c** sounds like a **k**, underline it. (Two are done for you.)

call   come   cent

(cider)   city   cat

cap   cane   cold

cinder   coat   cell

candy   cup   coin

                        cuff

Dollar Bank

Cut out the dollars with words that start with the same sound as .
Paste them in the dollar bank.

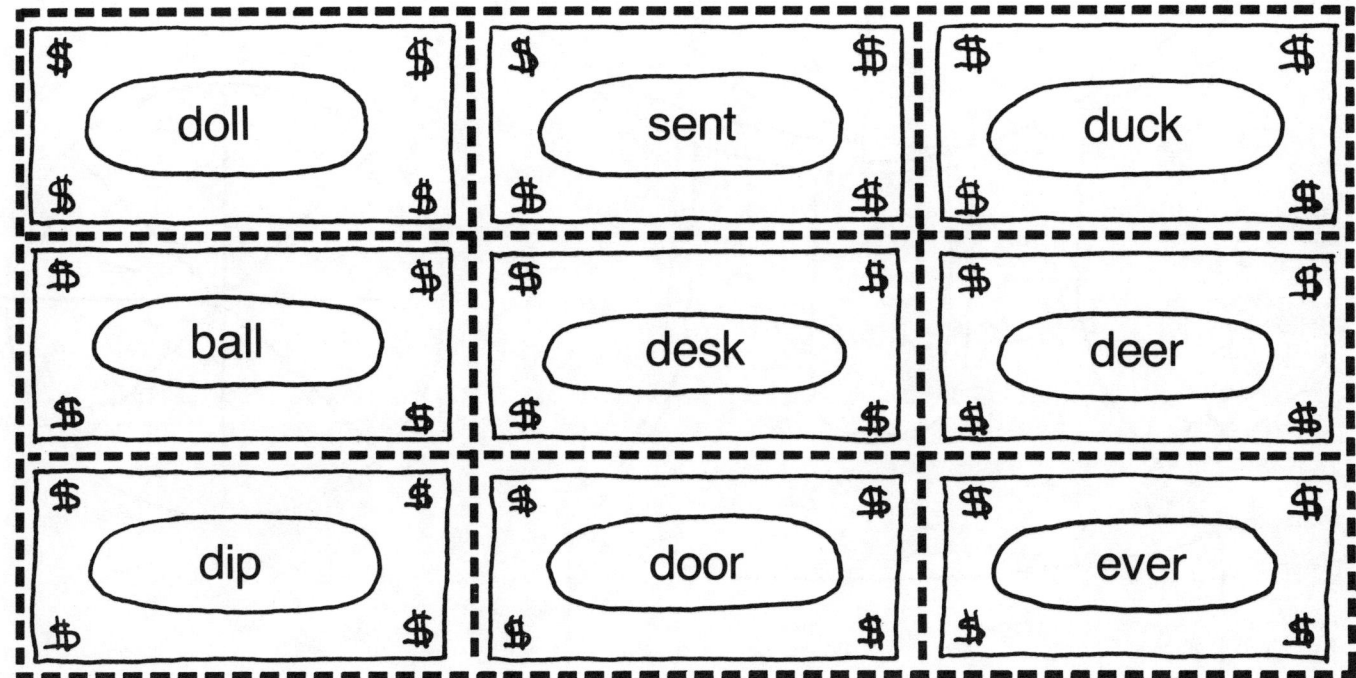

doll	sent	duck
ball	desk	deer
dip	door	ever

Name _____

A Fancy Fan

Cut out the fan. Cut out the small circle. Put a
paper fastener through the centers of both
circles. Move the small circle so you can read the
words.

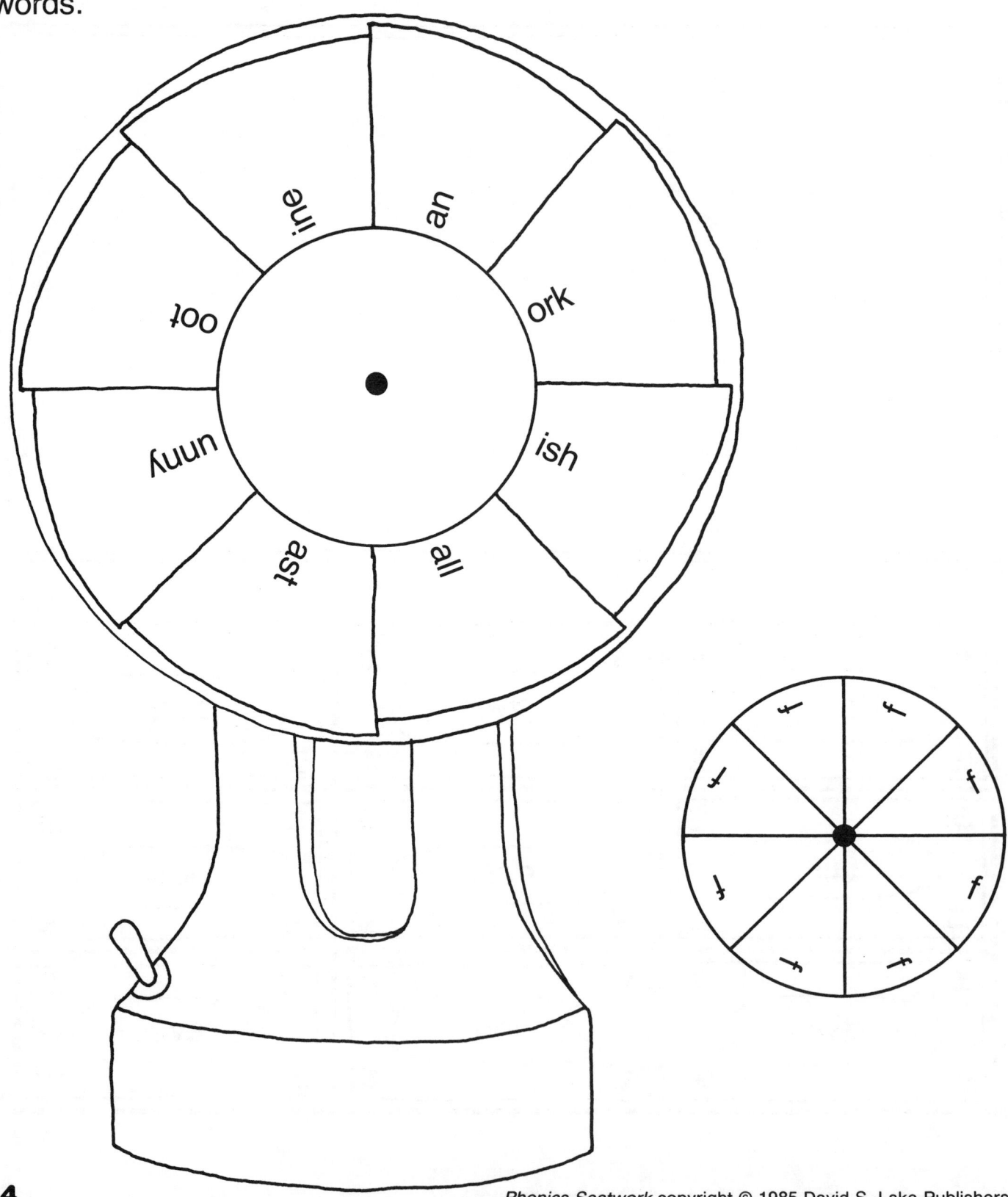

Magic Drawing

If the word has a hard **g**, color the shape yellow.
If the word has a soft **g**, color the shape any other color.

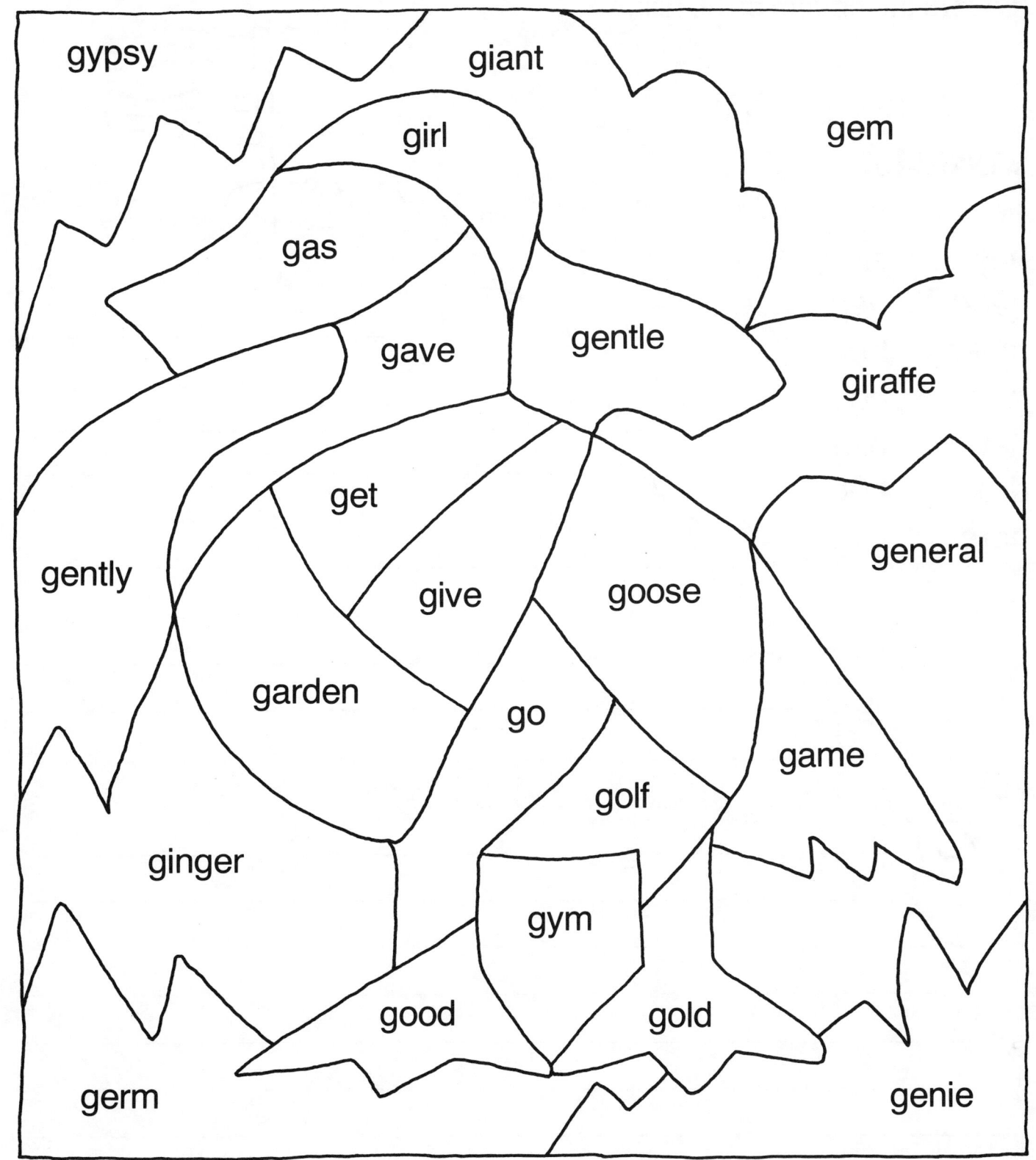

High on the Hill

Choose some words that
start with the same sound as .
Print them on the lines to reach the top of the hill.
(Start at the bottom of the hill.)

Word List

he	hill
has	live
hand	hen
make	heel
horn	hook
hat	nice
drop	hot
here	him

Fill the Jar!

Fill the jar with jellybeans! Cut along the
dotted lines. Cut out the jellybeans
with words that start with the same sound as .
Paste them in the jar.

Cut along dotted lines.

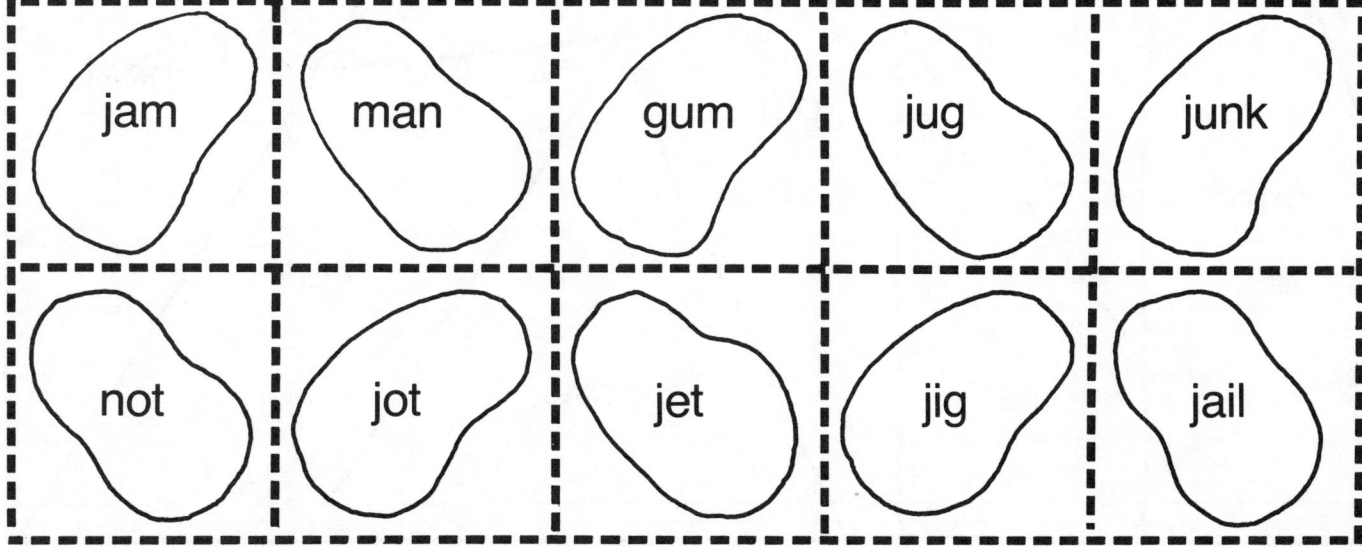

| jam | man | gum | jug | junk |
| not | jot | jet | jig | jail |

Mystery Picture

Find the words that start with the same sound as 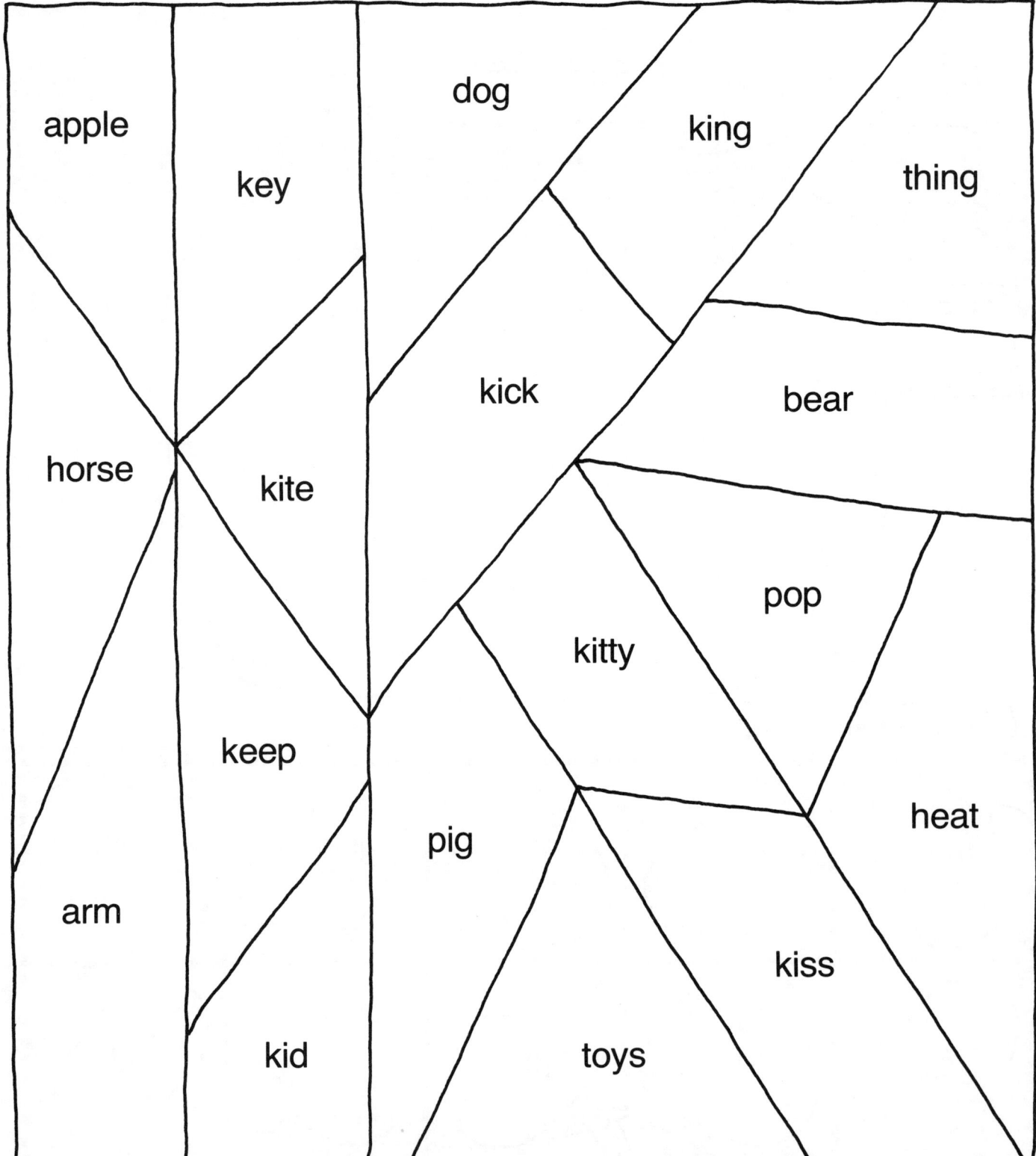.
Color those shapes red. Color the other shapes blue.

apple

dog

key

king

thing

kick

bear

horse

kite

pop

kitty

keep

heat

arm

pig

kiss

kid

toys

8

Name ______________________________ **l**

Look and Learn

Color the pictures that start with the same sound as .
Draw an X through the other pictures.

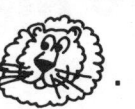

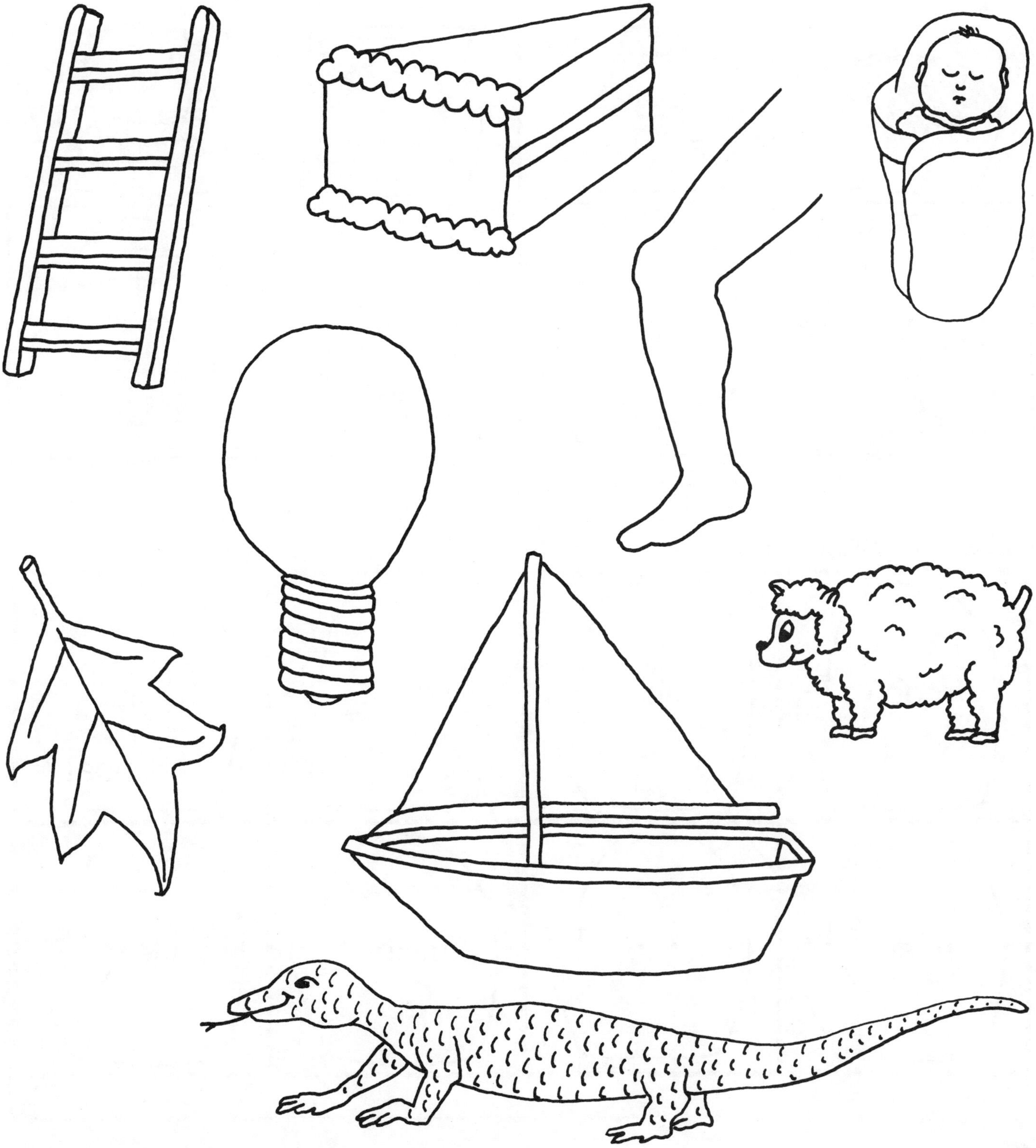

Match the Mittens

Cut out the mittens with words that start with the same sound as .
Paste them on the mittens with pictures that match.

Cut along dotted lines.

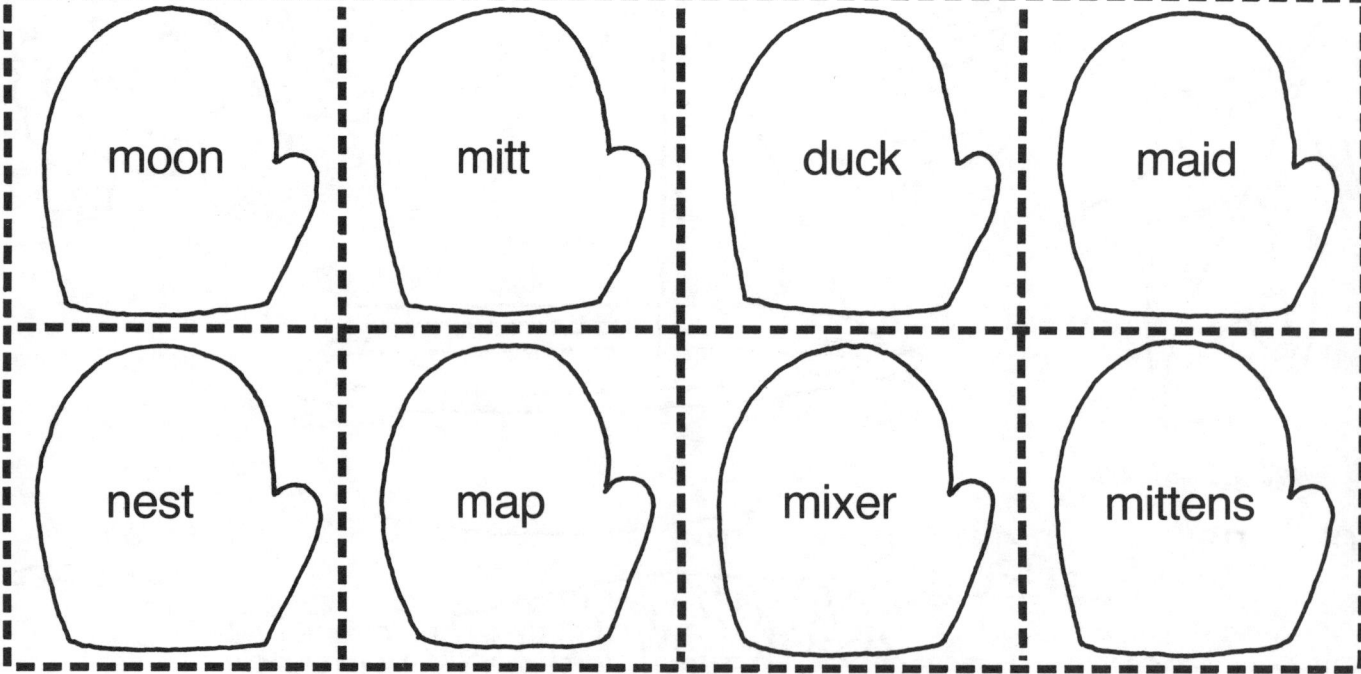

moon	mitt	duck	maid
nest	map	mixer	mittens

No, No, No!

What do you *not* like? Write about what you would say "No!" to. Use some words that start with the same sound as ⌇⌇⌇ .

_____

- -

_____

- -

_____

- -

_____

- -

_____

- -

_____

- -

_____

Word List

not   name   nest   nap   map   news   no   neat

pin   nut   nine   nail   neck   nag   hat   nose

noise   mouse   needle   never   need   number

Pick a Picture

Find a picture in a magazine of
something whose name begins with the same sound as 🦚 .
Cut the picture out, and paste it on this paper.
Write a story about the picture, using as many **p**
words as you can.

_____

_ _ _ _ _ _ _ _ _ _ _ _ _ _

_____

_ _ _ _ _ _ _ _ _ _ _ _ _ _

_____

_ _ _ _ _ _ _ _ _ _ _ _ _ _

_____

_ _

_____

_ _

_____

_ _

_____

Word List

pie	yellow	pin	pail	pick	paw	pig	page
dime	pan	pull	pain	paint	pair	part	dog
pet	paper	park	pot	rug	pipe	pen	

Quilting Party

Read each word below. If the word starts with the same sound as 👑 ,
color the square blue. Color the other squares
any way you like.

quick	tiger	quilt	pencil	quail	glass
berry	quiet	yours	quake	fly	quart
quit	tape	queen	desk	quote	stripe
tree	quiz	radio	quarter	jar	question

Name ______________________________ **r**

Rake the Leaves!

On the leaves, print words that start with the same sound as .
Color the leaves. Finish the picture.

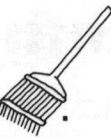

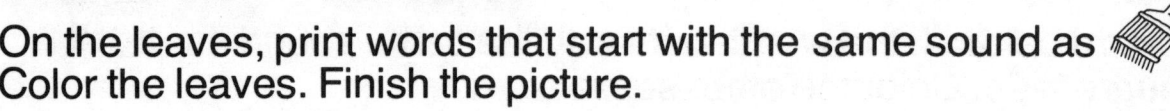

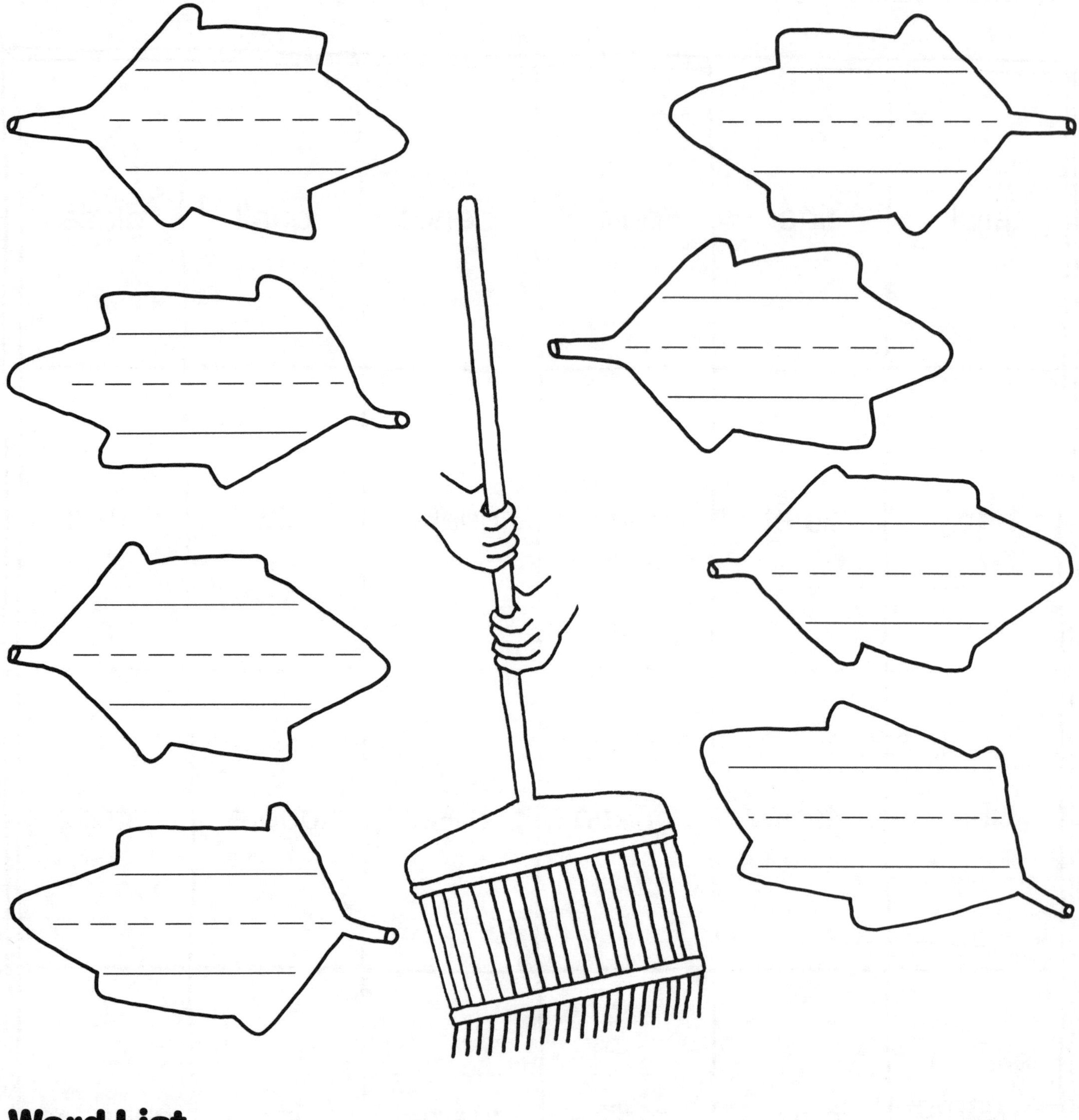

Word List

red	read	pan	ran	ring	nut	rabbit	ride
rose	rug	tape	rain	roof	rope	rake	rib

Something Starts with S

Something in this picture starts with **s**. See what it is! Find the words that start with the same sound as 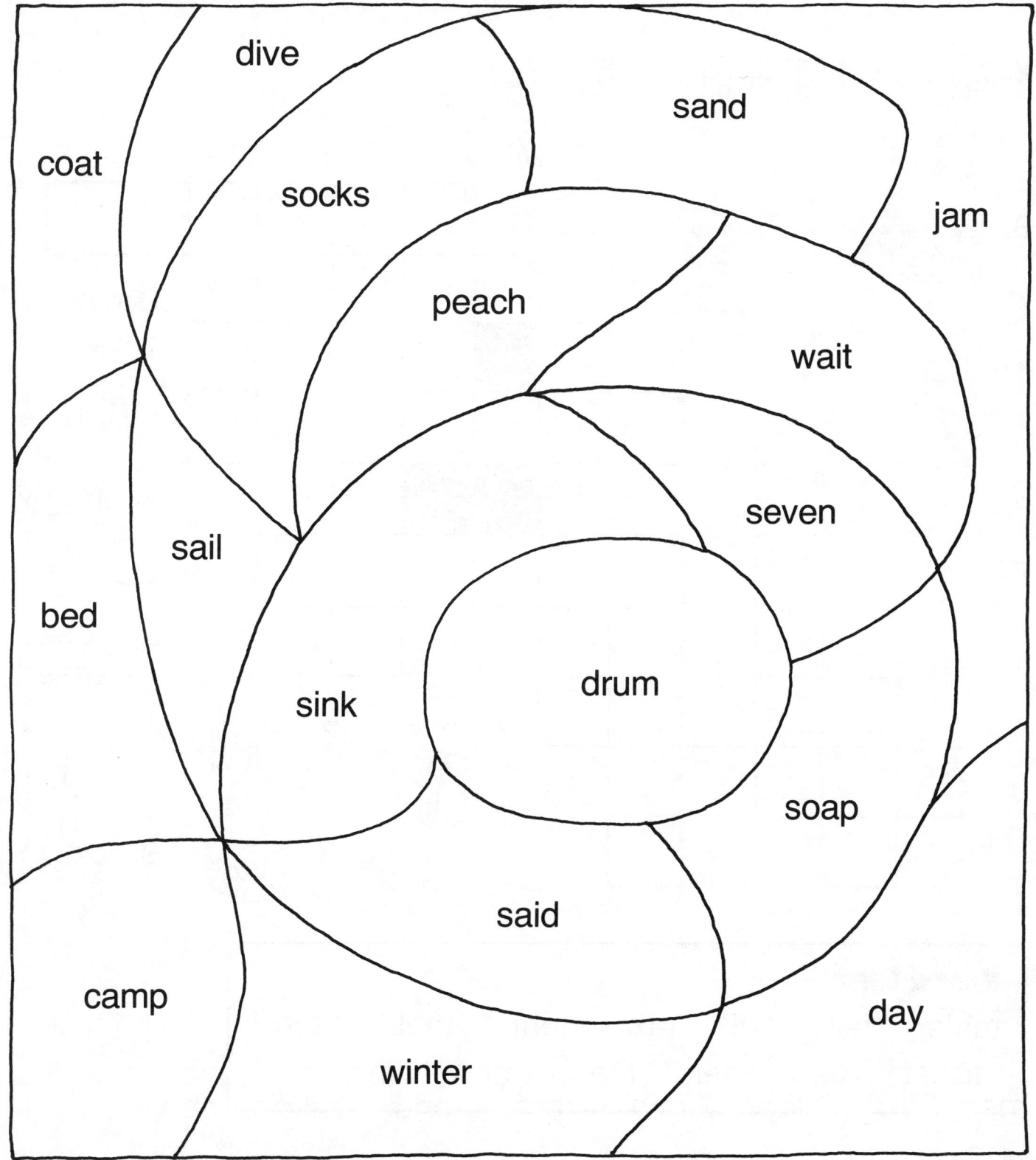. Color those shapes green. Color the other shapes a different color.

dive

coat

sand

socks

jam

peach

wait

seven

sail

bed

sink

drum

soap

said

camp

day

winter

T Time!

Look at the picture. Match each picture with a word from the list. Print the word in the puzzle.

Across

2.

3.

5.

8.

9.

10.

Down

1.

2.

4.

6.

7.

8.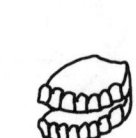

9.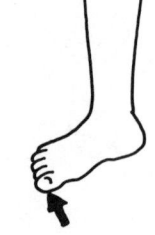

Word List

table   tail   tall   taxi   tear   teeth   ten

ticket   tie   tiger   toe   top   tulip

A Twisting Vine

Find the leaves with words that start with the same sound as 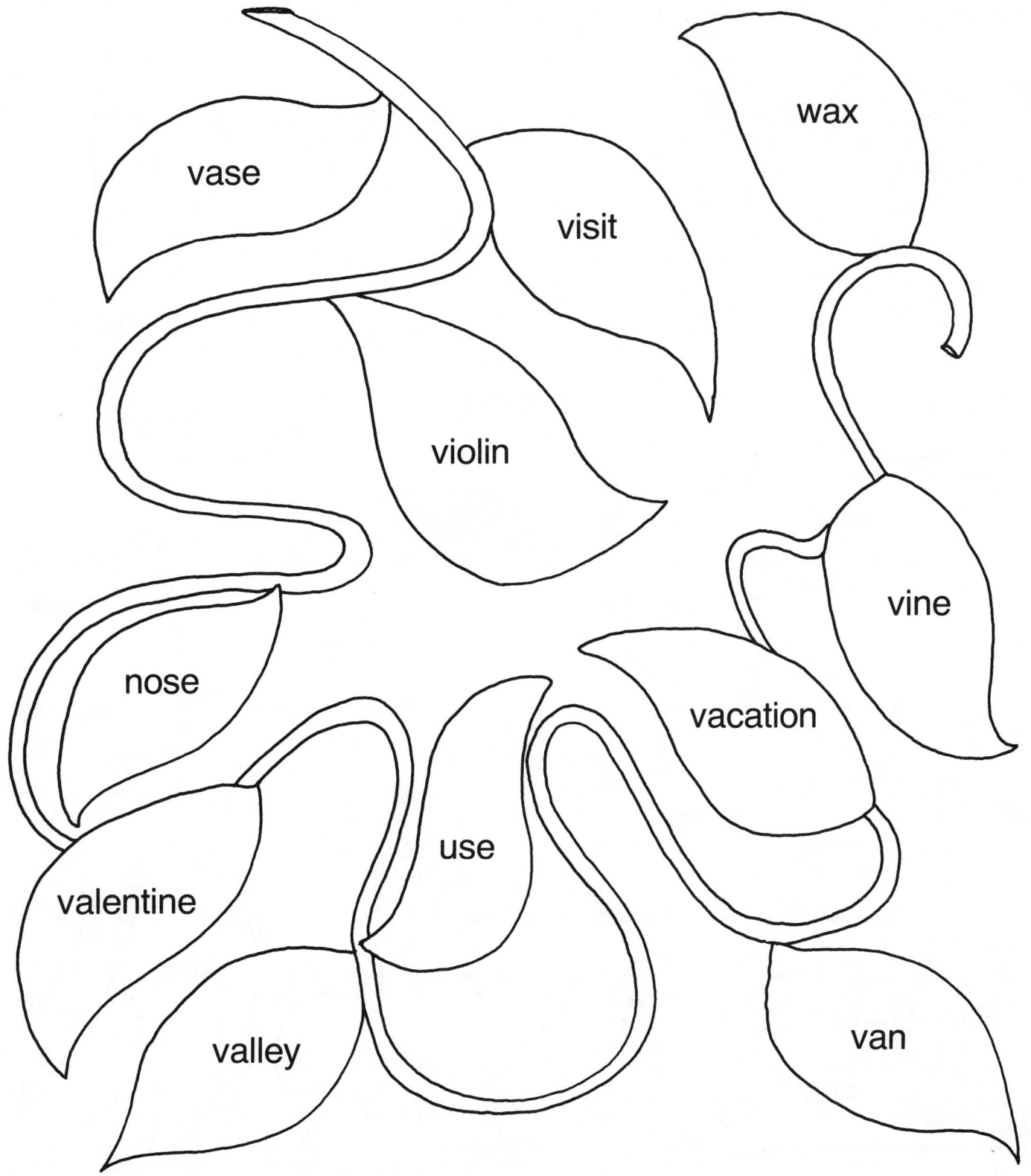.
Color those leaves green. Color the other leaves brown.

wax

vase

visit

violin

vine

nose

vacation

valentine

use

van

valley

Wide and Wild Wings

Find the wings with words that start with the same sound as .
Color those birds blue. Color the other birds a
different color.

wind

web

week

meet

nest

wet

west

true

won

The Box That Was X-Rayed

If you could x-ray this box, what
would you see? Circle the words with the sound at the end of 6.

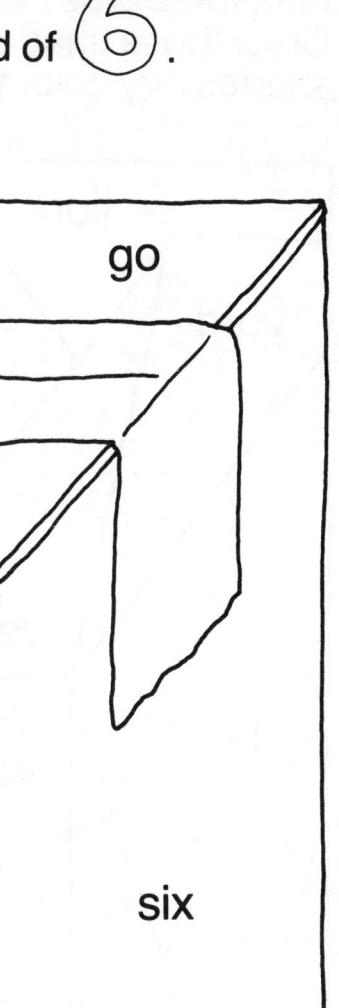

box   go

fill   wax

fox   six

ax   ox

tax

mix   man

A Page for the Y's

Find the words that start with the same sound as 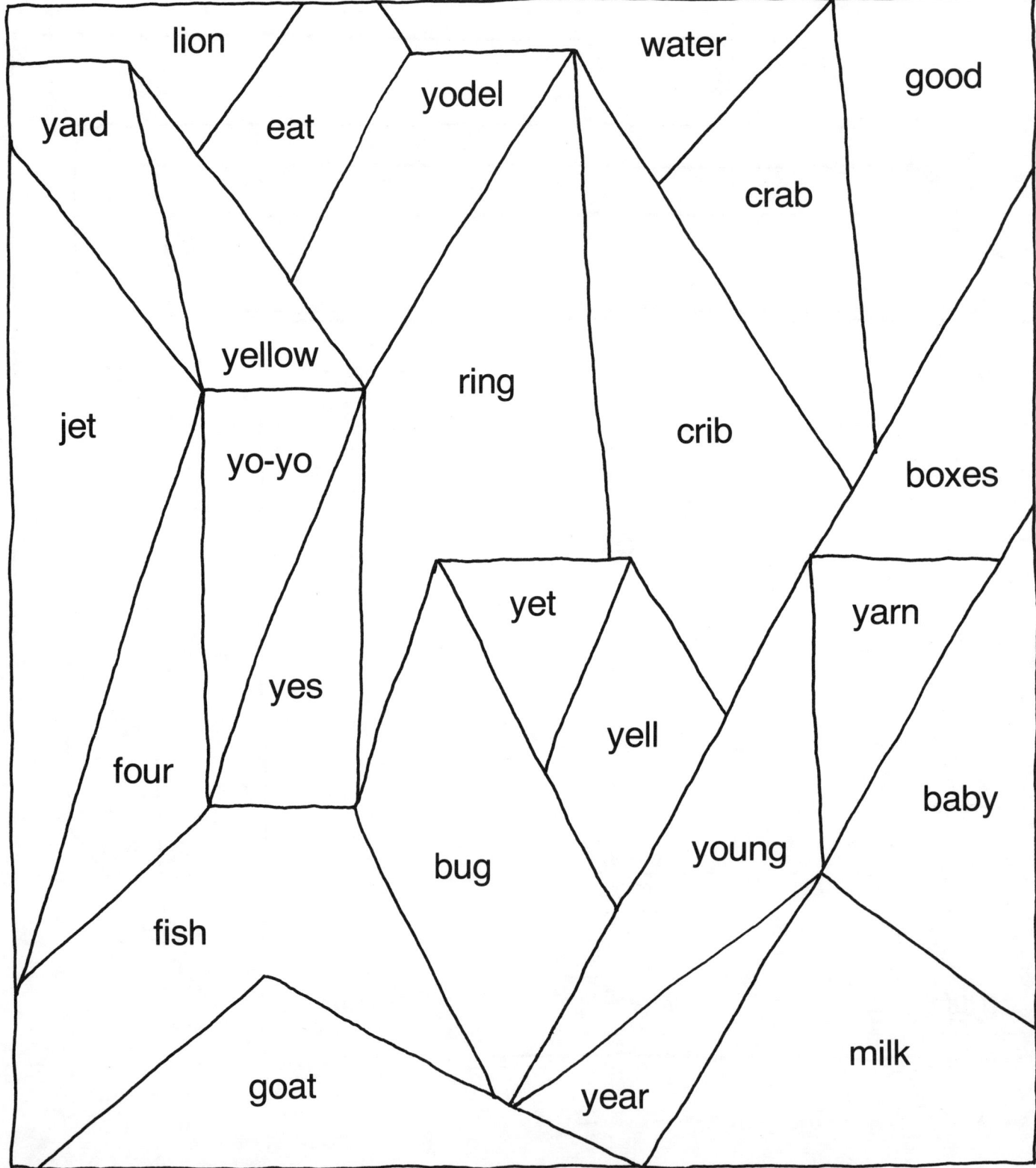.
Color those shapes yellow. Color the other
shapes any color you want.

lion
yard
eat
yodel
water
good
crab
yellow
jet
ring
yo-yo
crib
boxes
yet
yarn
yes
yell
four
baby
young
bug
fish
goat
year
milk

Phonics Seatwork copyright © 1985 David S. Lake Publishers

Zip the Zipper!

On the zipper spaces,
print words that start with the same sound as 🦓.

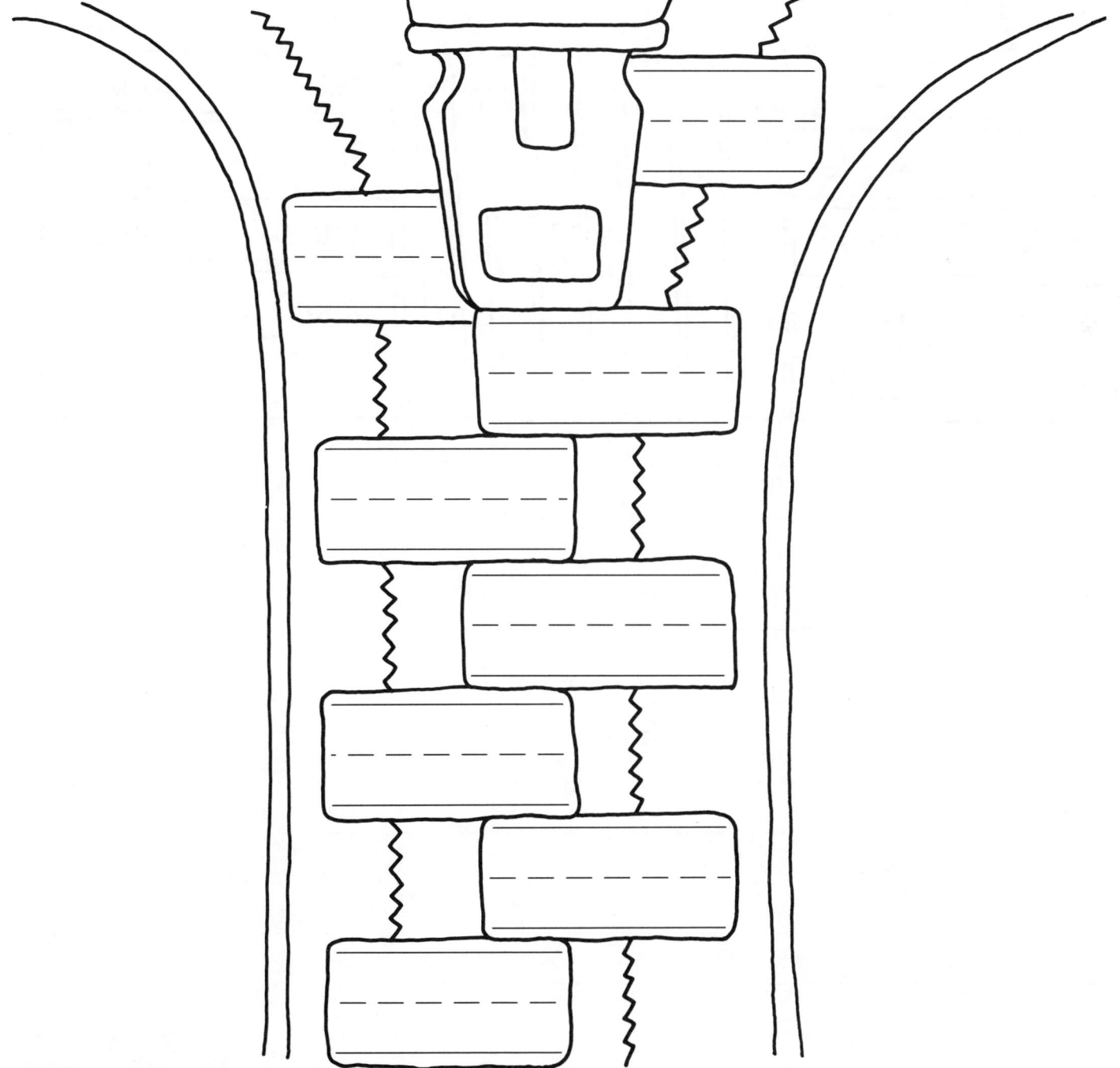

Word List

zoo   sun   zone   zebra   zoom   sand   zipper
zip   zero   zap   nap   zest   zing   safe

Name ______________________________ ā

A Day Behind the Gate

Write about what is behind the gate. Use some words that have the same vowel sound as .

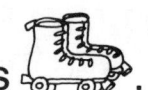

came	game
frame	wade
make	save
shake	rake
fan	bake

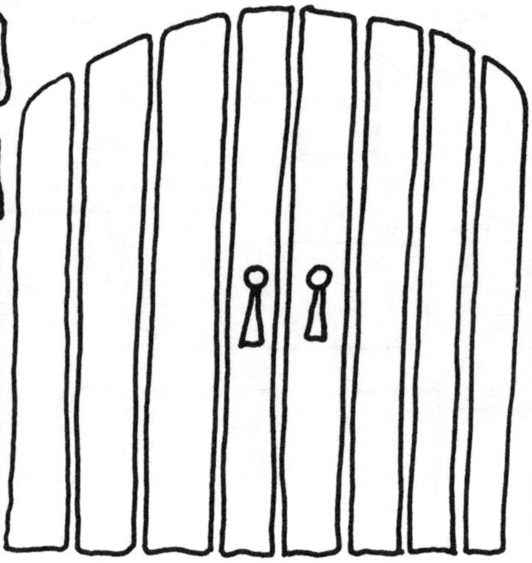

fat	tame
name	van
cane	mole
lake	vase
bone	lane

The Leaf Family

Write about the lives of the Leaf Family. Use
some words that have the same vowel sound as .

_____

- -

_____

- -

_____

- -

_____

- -

_____

Word List

feed	seem	see	send	peep	wee	men
mean	stem	team	reed	weep	leaf	meat
met	feet	felt	steam	sleeve	rest	bet	jeep
ten	tease	beep	leap	belt	need	steep

Name ______________________________

Help the Vines Grow

On the long ī vine, print words with the same vowel sound as .

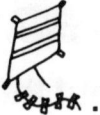

On the short ĭ vine, print words with the same vowel sound as .

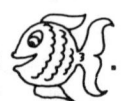

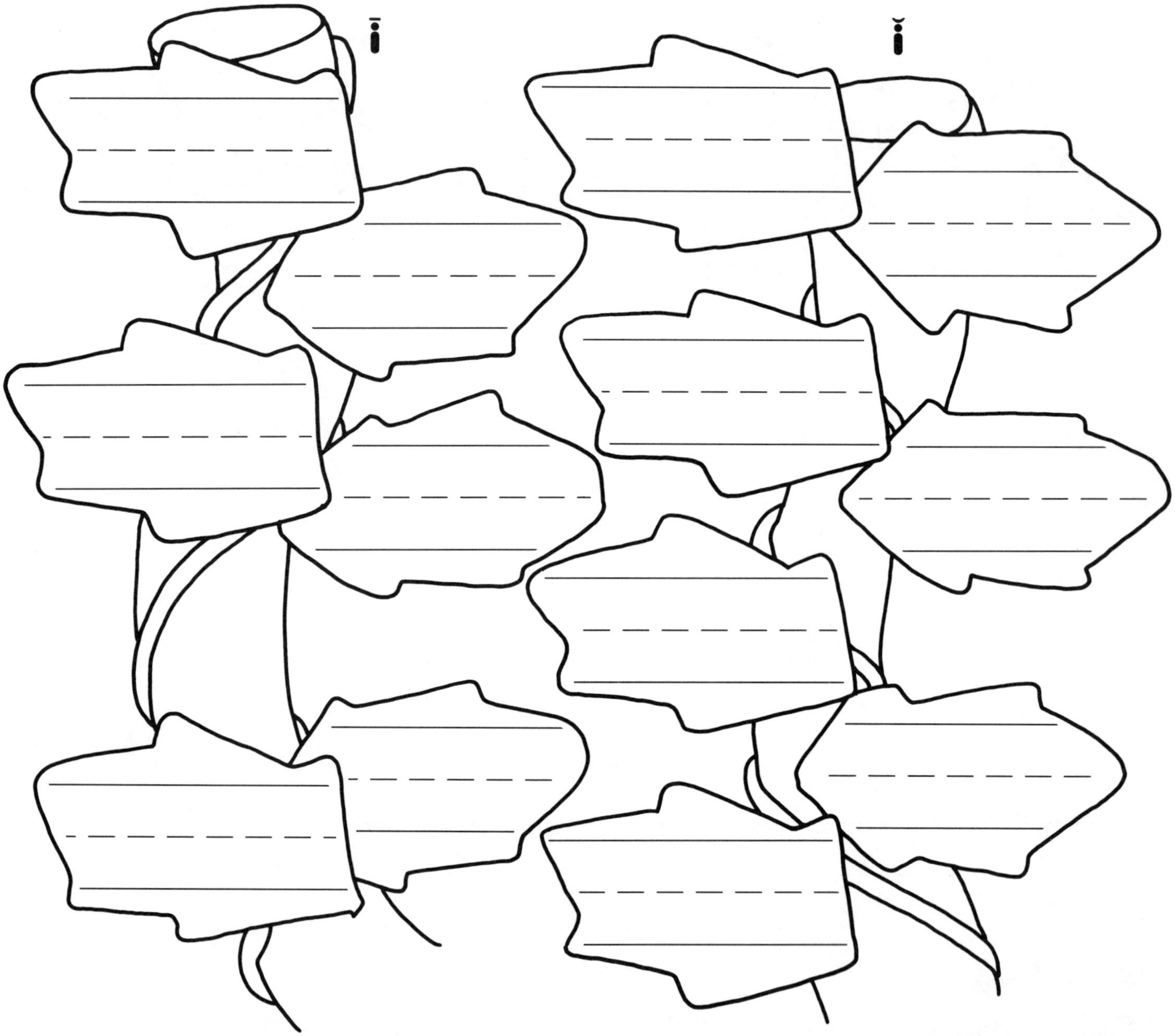

Word List

lid wig mice gift pile pit bike kite fine
pick kid kit pine pipe dig hill like dime

Fill in the Words

Look at the picture or read the clue. Match each picture or clue with words from the word list to do the puzzle.

Across

1.

3.

5.

7.

8.

Down

1.

2.

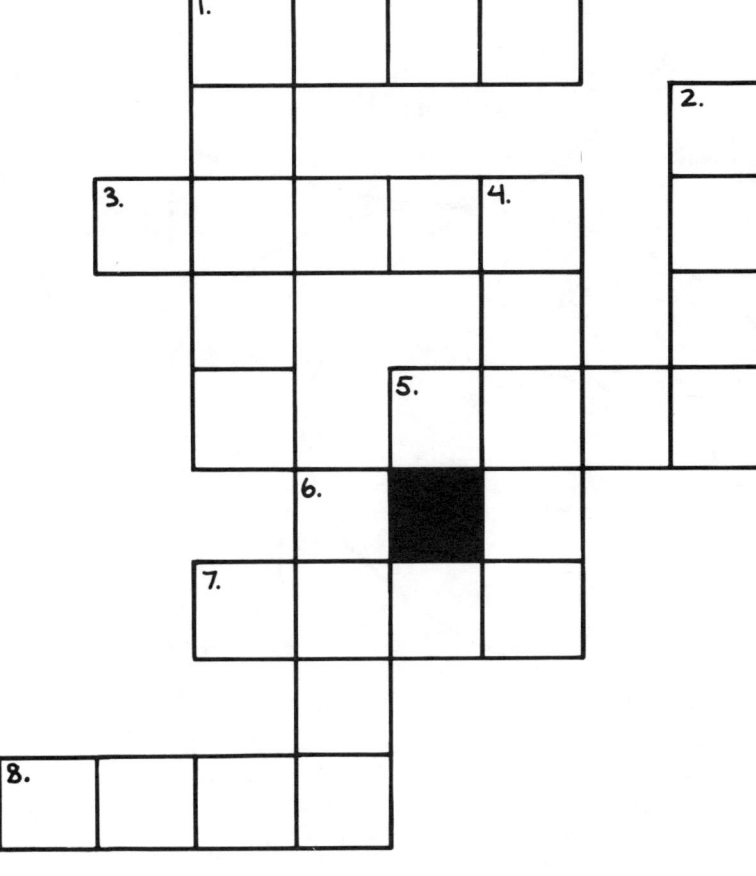

4. A small rock is called a _____ .

6.

Word List

bones	cone	home	nose	note
phone	pole	rope	stone	

This Makes Music

If the shape has a word with the same vowel sound as , color it blue.

If the shape has a word with the same vowel sound as , color it another color.

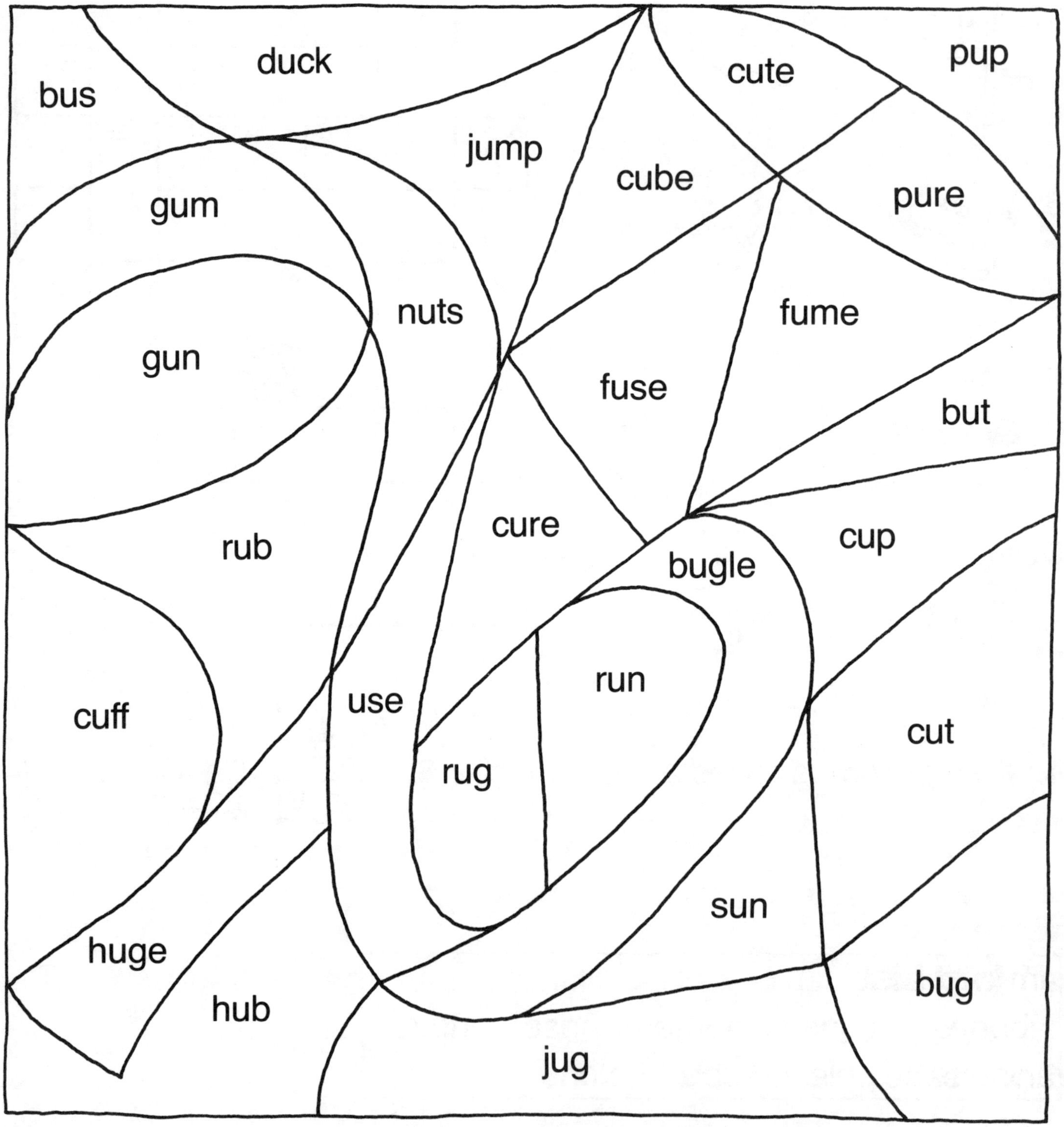

duck

bus

cute

pup

jump

cube

gum

pure

nuts

fume

gun

fuse

but

rub

cure

cup

bugle

cuff

run

cut

use

rug

huge

sun

hub

bug

jug

The Boy with the Cap

Write a story about the boy who wears
the cap. Use words with the same vowel sound as  .

_____

– – – – – – – – – – – – – – – – –

_____

– – – – – – – – – – – – – – – – –

_____

– – – – – – – – – – – – – – – – –

_____

– – – – – – – – – – – – – – – – –

_____

– – – – – – – – – – – – – – – – –

_____

– – – – – – – – – – – – – – – – –

_____

– – – – – – – – – – – – – – – – –

Word List

jam	lad	lap	camp	lane	ant	bad	trade
back	and	had	ham	hate	hat	pal	pale
ran	sane	sand	plan				

Name ______________________________ ĕ

Ring the Bell

Write about the things you like to do when the school bell rings. Use some words with the same vowel sound as .

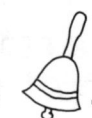

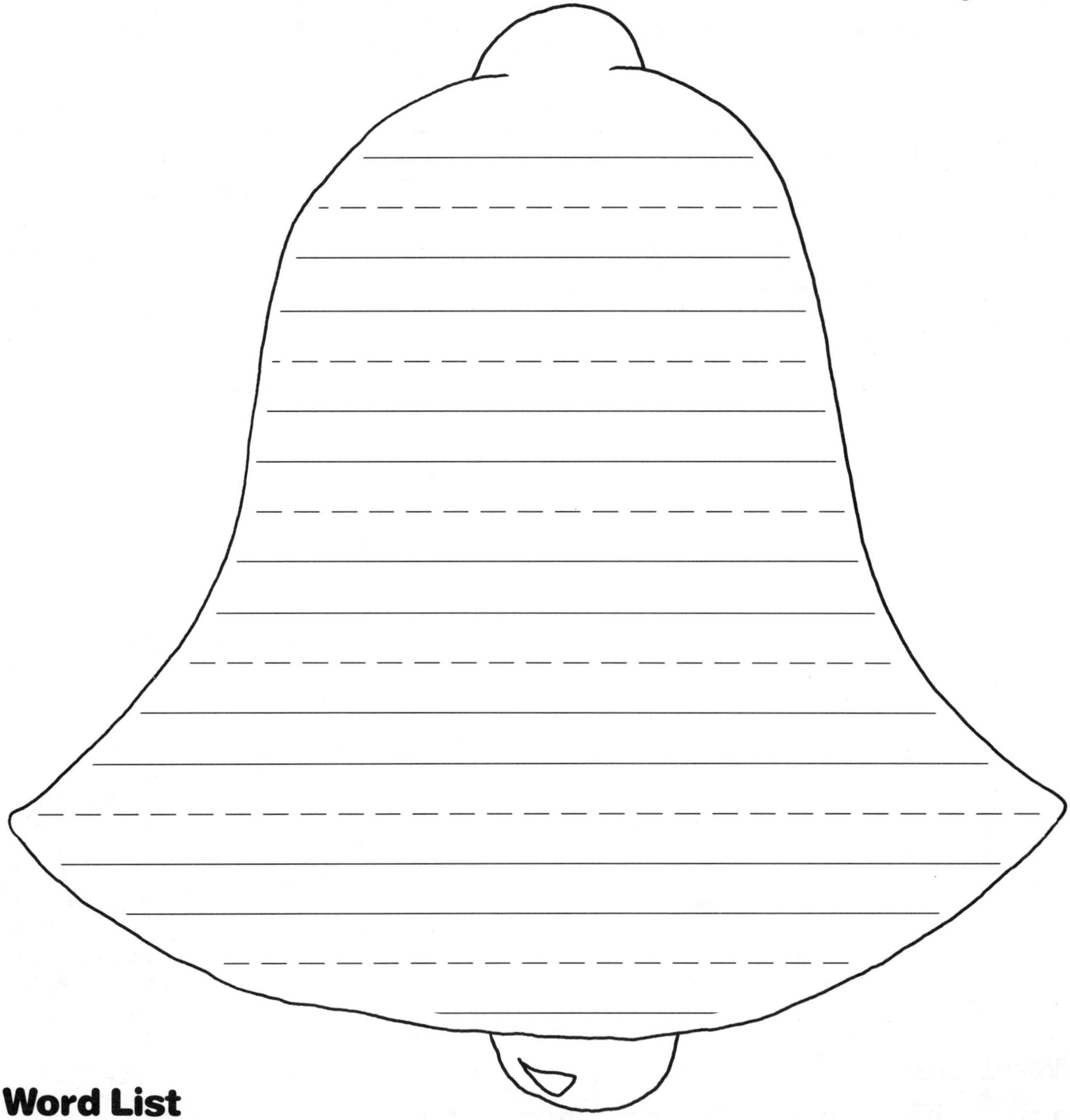

Word List

tent	sled	beg	belt	sell	smell	dream
egg	leg	key	best	send	desk	dress
bean	bend	nest	lean	tell	den	

Fill the Glass with Milk!

In the word list, find words with the same vowel sound as .
Print them on the glass and on the pitcher.

Word List

fin   pin   six   pine   sing   sit   fig   lid   wing

sink   hid   big   hide   ring   mitt   pig   pile

milk   hill   lift   pick   mix   pill   time   tin

Phonics Seatwork copyright © 1985 David S. Lake Publishers

Follow the Dots!

Start at the star. Follow the short ŏ words. Draw
a line from dot to dot in order, skipping the dots
with long ō words.

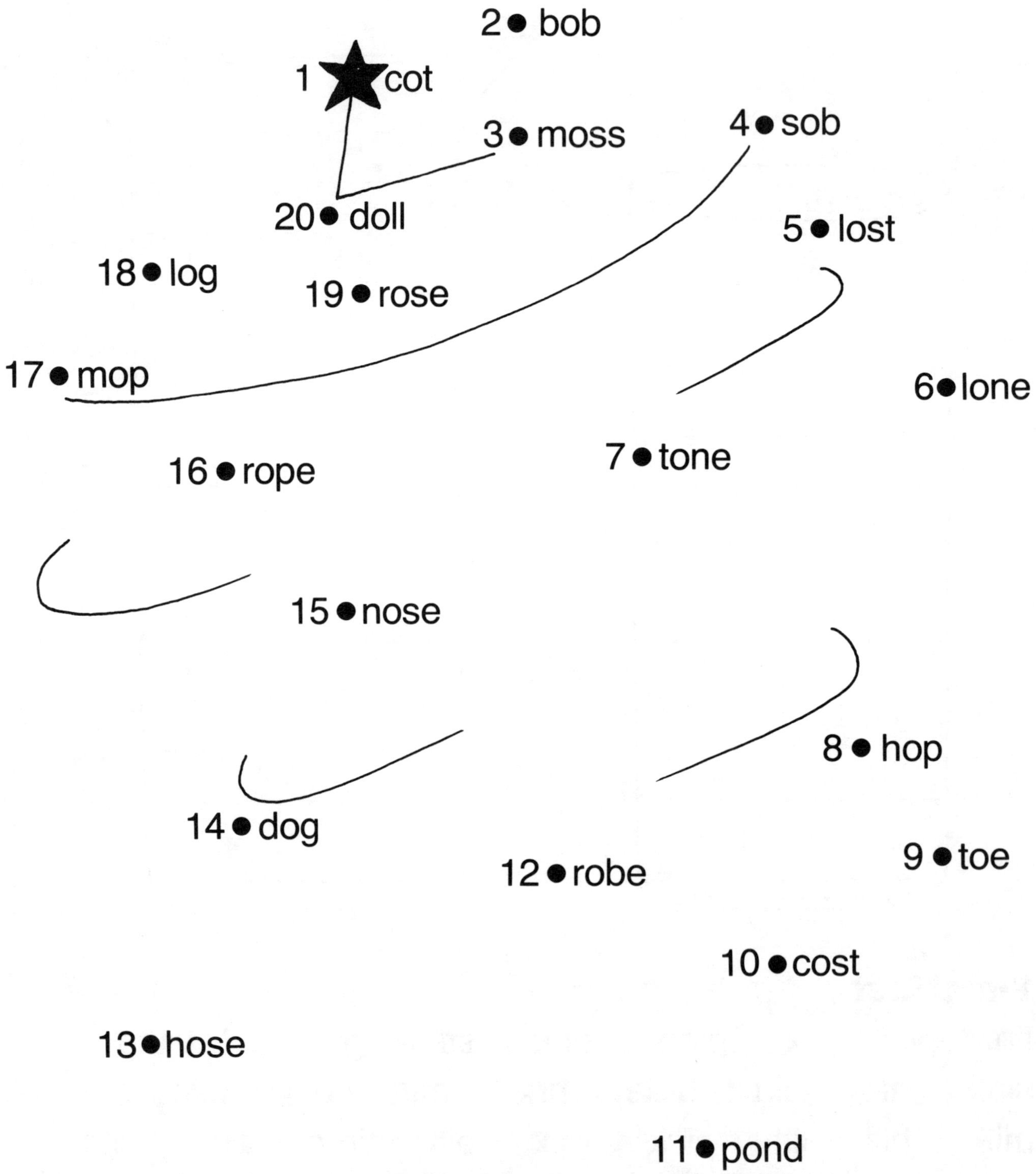

2● bob

1 ★ cot

3● moss   4● sob

20● doll

5● lost

18● log   19● rose

6●lone

17●mop

7● tone

16 ● rope

15●nose

8 ● hop

14● dog

9 ● toe

12● robe

10 ● cost

13●hose

11●pond

A Puzzle for Fun

Print short **ŭ** words on the puzzle pieces. Cut out the pieces along the dotted lines, and place them on a piece of construction paper. When you have the puzzle together, paste the pieces down.

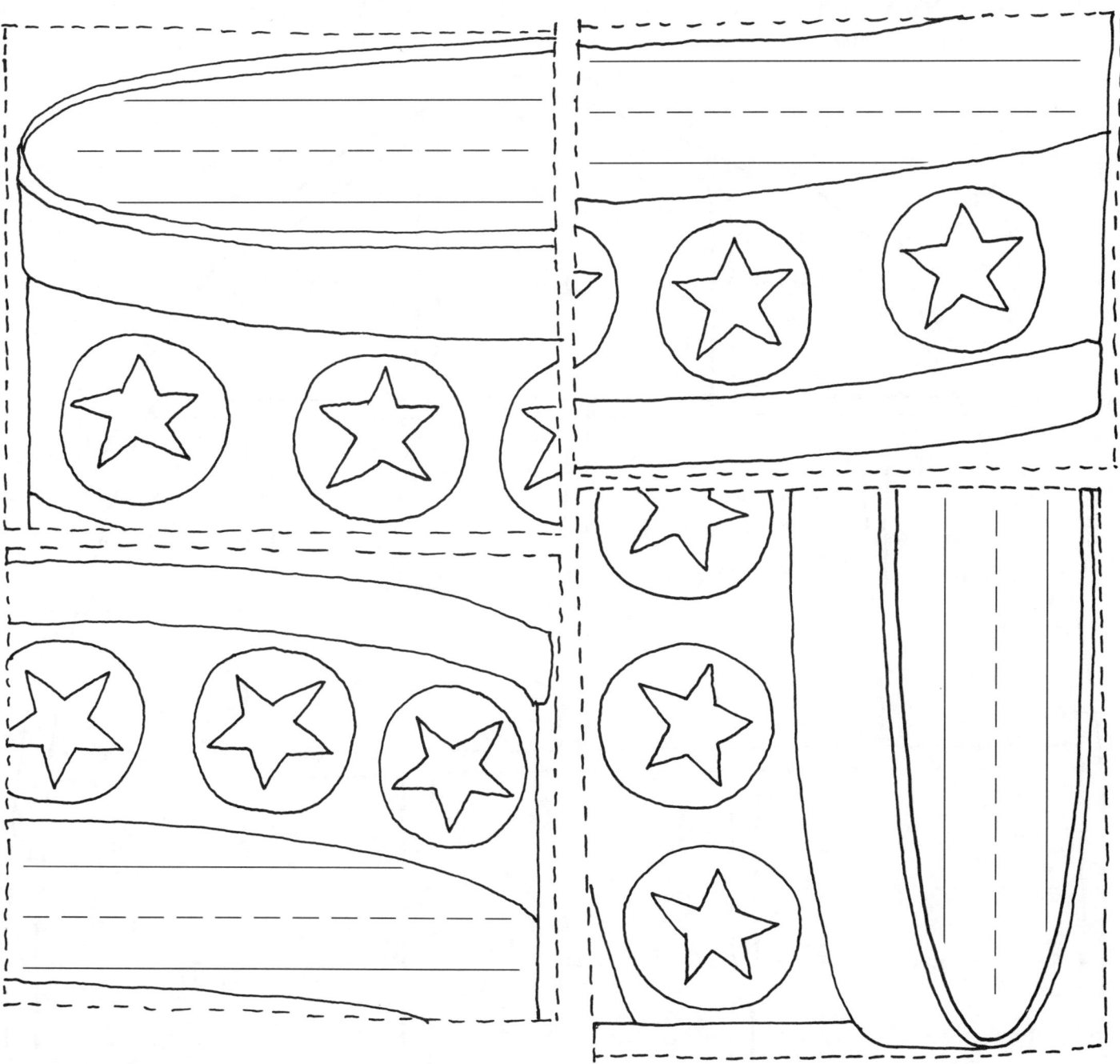

Word List

duck   bug   cut   cup   run   cute   sun   pup   must

rub   drum   fun   tulip   dust   gum   blue   lunch

Stained Glass Window

Make a pretty stained glass window.
Find the sections with words
that have the same vowel sound as 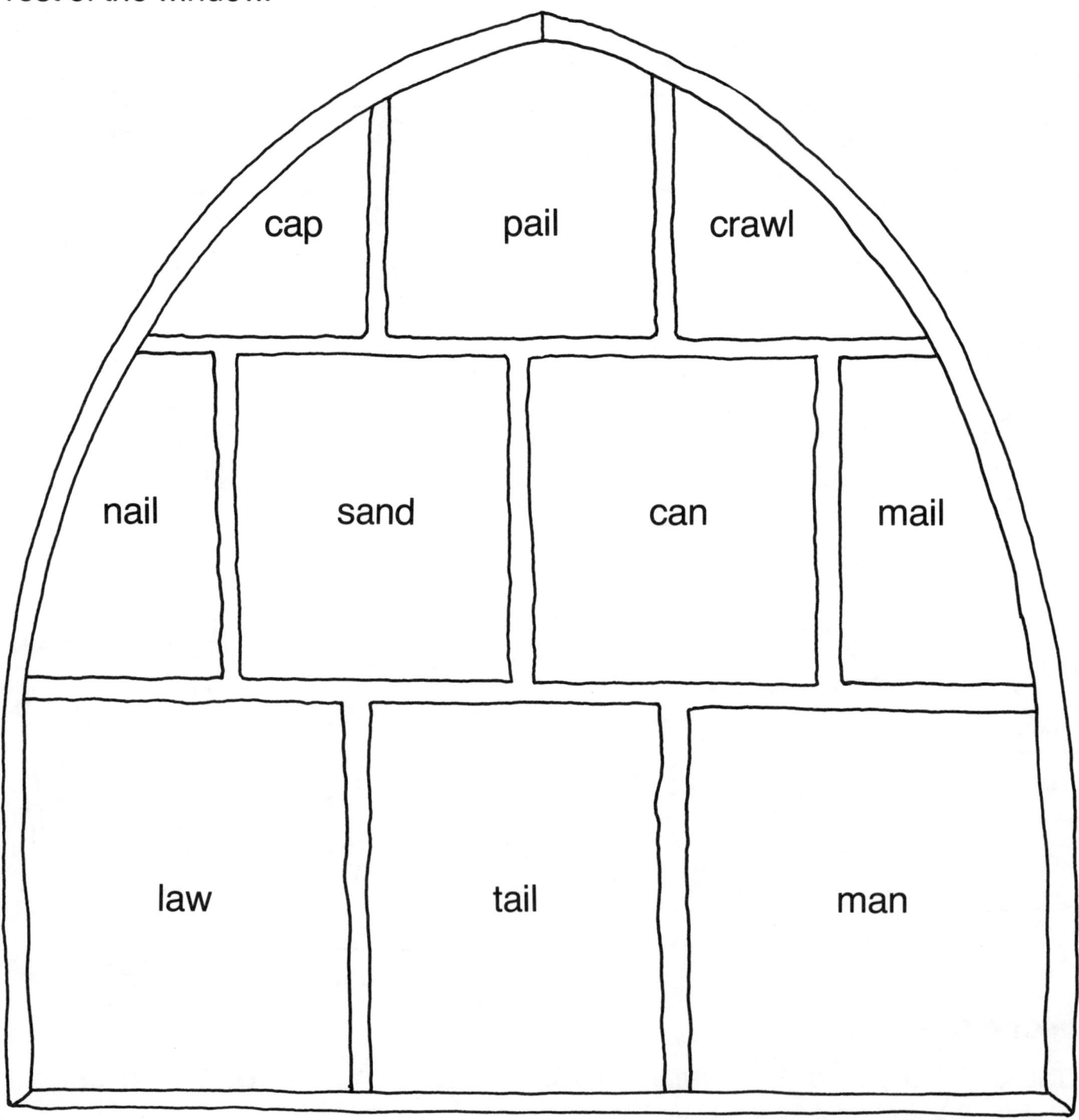 .
Color those sections red.
Use other colors for the
rest of the window.

cap

pail

crawl

nail

sand

can

mail

law

tail

man

Name _____

Find the Way

Help Jay find his way home! Find all the
spaces that have words with the same vowel sound as .
Color them red. Color the rest of the picture in
other colors.

bay

may

way

talk

mat

sat

wall

lay

sad

cap

gray

pan

ray

tall

nag

rat

pay

day

hay

gay

Name ______________________________ **oa**

Coast Along

Coast down the hill!
Starting at the top, print words with the same vowel sound as .

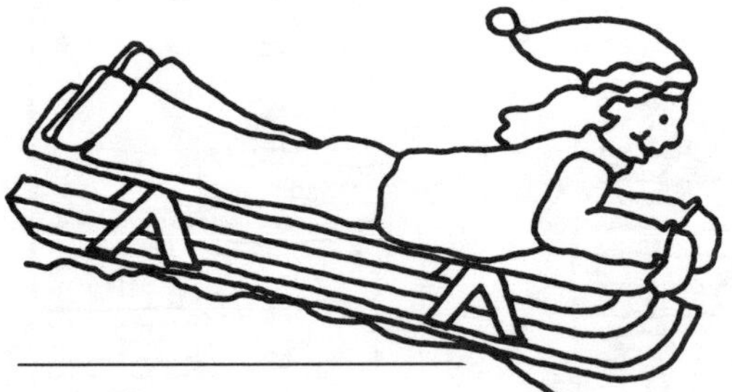

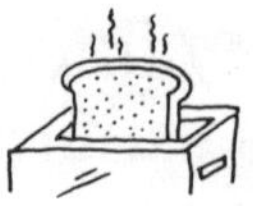

Word List

soap	toad
coat	toss
cost	goat
boat	road
loan	moan
mob	coal
load	dock

Uptown and Downtown in My Town

Finish the story. Use some words with the **ow** sound as in .

The town I live in

Word List

how   cow   owl   howl   crow   crowd   crown   flow

glow   town   clown   down   flower   frown   tower

Show Me a Rainbow

Finish the story. Use some words that have the **ow** sound as in 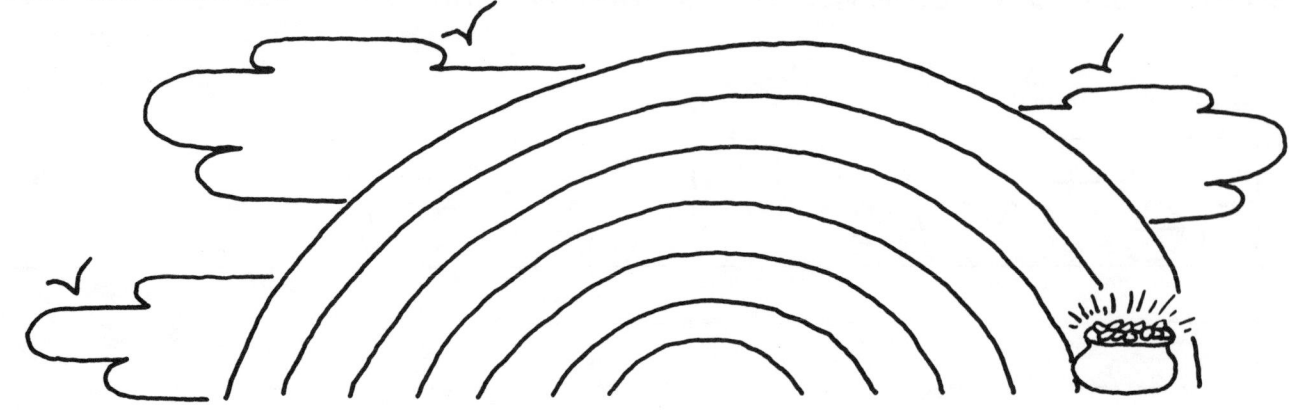.
Color the rainbow.

At the end of the rainbow,

_____

_____

_____

_____

_____

_____

_____

_____

Word List

rainbow	crowd	low	mow	cow	sow	town
bowl	crow	slow	grow	arrow	elbow	below
blow	flow	frown	glow	how	row	tow

Phonics Seatwork copyright © 1985 David S. Lake Publishers

Name ______________________________ **ou**

What's He Shouting About?

This man is shouting! What's it about?
Use some words with the **ou** sound as in .

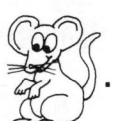

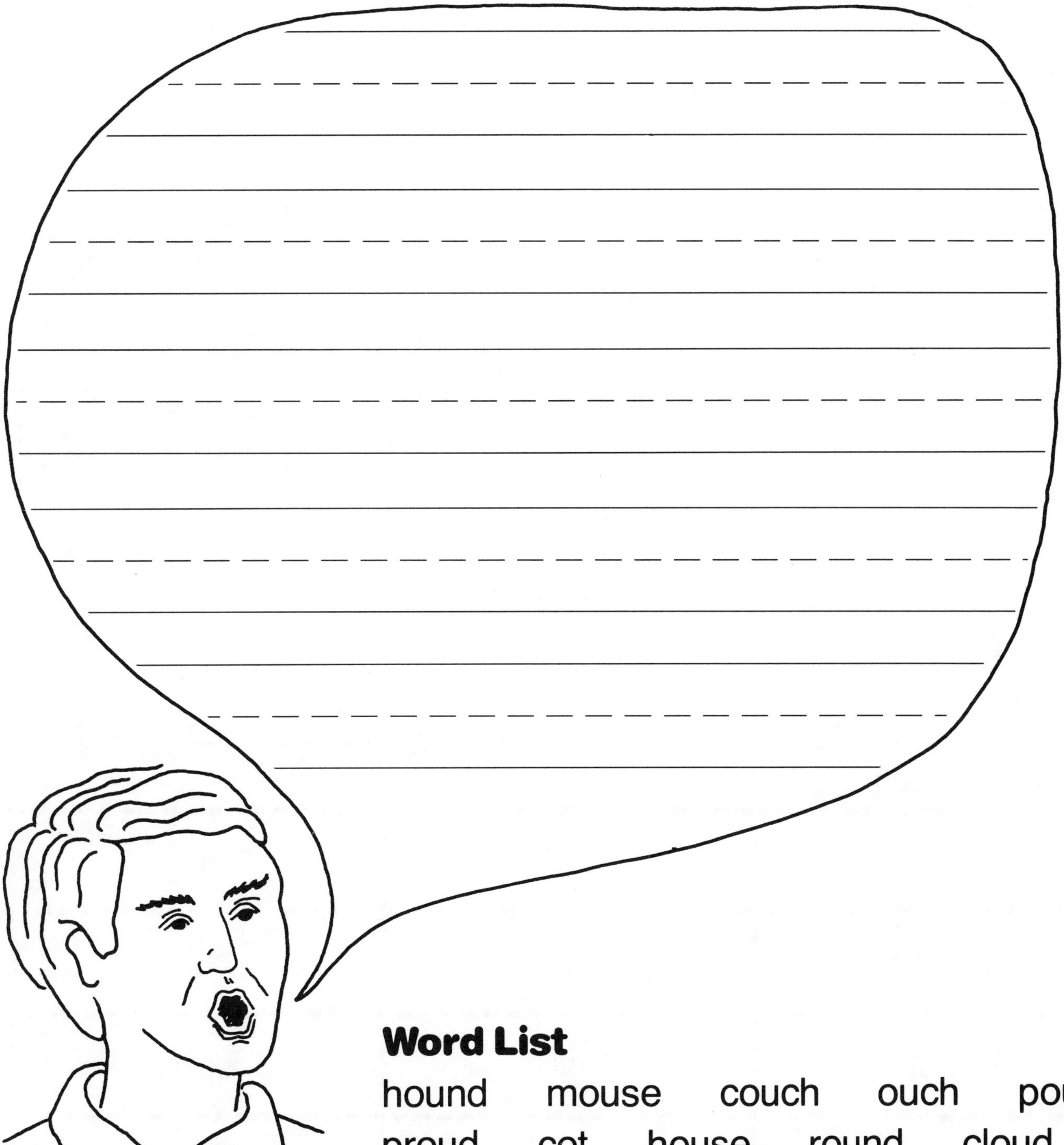

Word List

hound mouse couch ouch pouch
proud cot house round cloud
out trot trout pout put

What's Boiling?

Materials Needed: cotton balls, scissors, paste

Cut out the words with the **oi** sound as in .
Paste the words on cotton balls.
Paste the balls to the paper, as if they
are coming out of the teapot.

Cut along dotted lines.

boil	bowl	soil
poison	spool	coin
moist	foil	spoil
oil	pool	toil

   Phonics Seatwork copyright © 1985 David S. Lake Publishers

Name _____

Jump for Joy!

Help the boys, Roy and Troy, jump for joy.
On the lines, print words that have the **oy** sound as in  .

_____

- -

_____

- -

_____

- -

_____

- -

_____

Word List

boy   play   joy   Roy   Jay   Troy   toy
royal   voyage   day   enjoy   clay

39

Fill the Balloons

On the balloons, print words with the oo sound as in .
Color the picture.

Word List

moon   shoot   hood   look   room   soon   shook

hook   wood   broom   boom   tooth   spoon   cool

cook   pool   coop   fool   hoop   took   zoom

   Phonics Seatwork copyright © 1985 David S. Lake Publishers

A New Kind of Stew

Cut out the words that have the **ew** sound. Paste them in the stew pot.

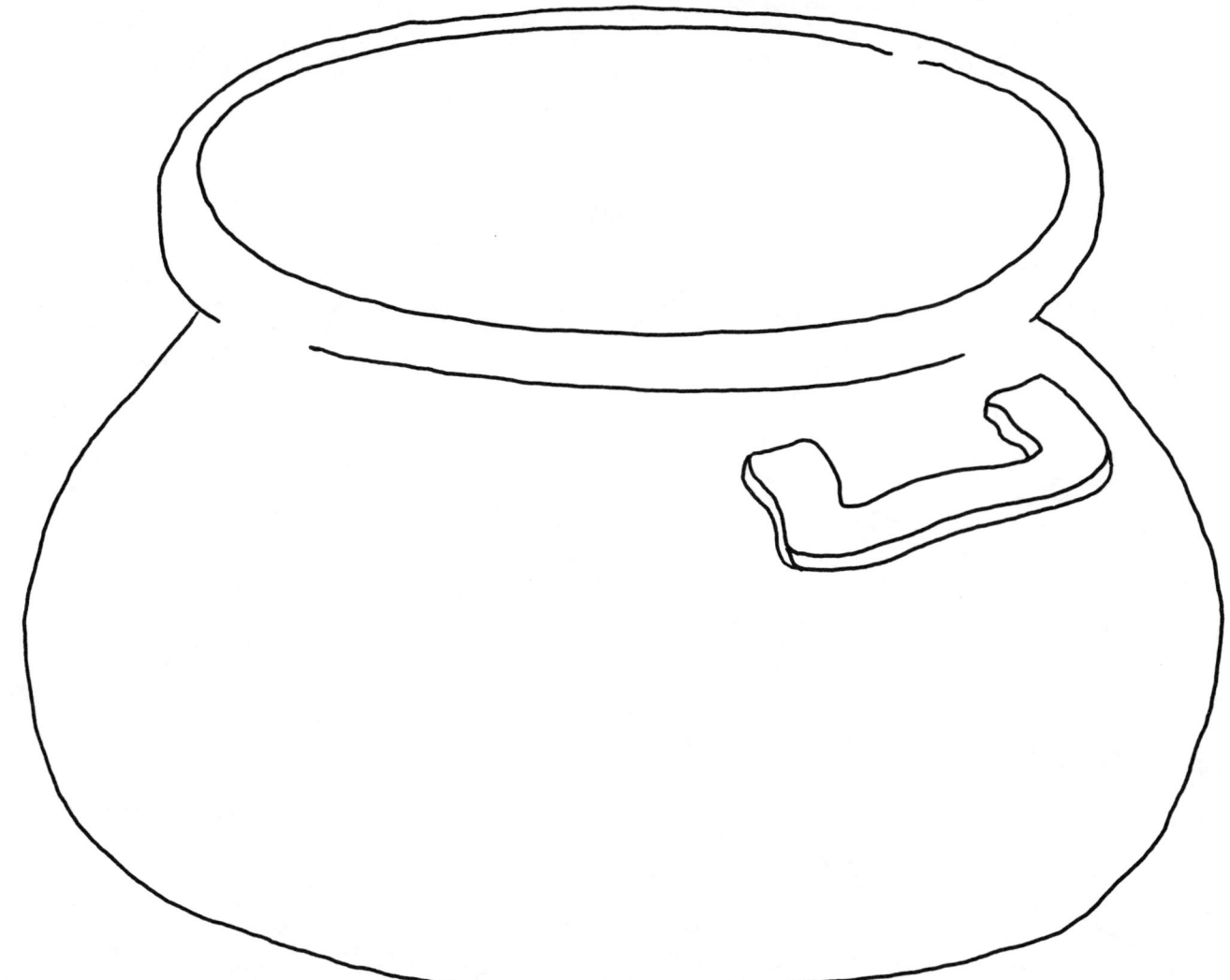

Cut along dotted lines.

flow	threw	chew
blow	blew	new
stew	down	crow
brown	drew	flew

The Autumn Leaves Are Falling

Find the leaves that have words with the **au**
sound on them. Color them red. Color the other
leaves yellow. Color the branches green.

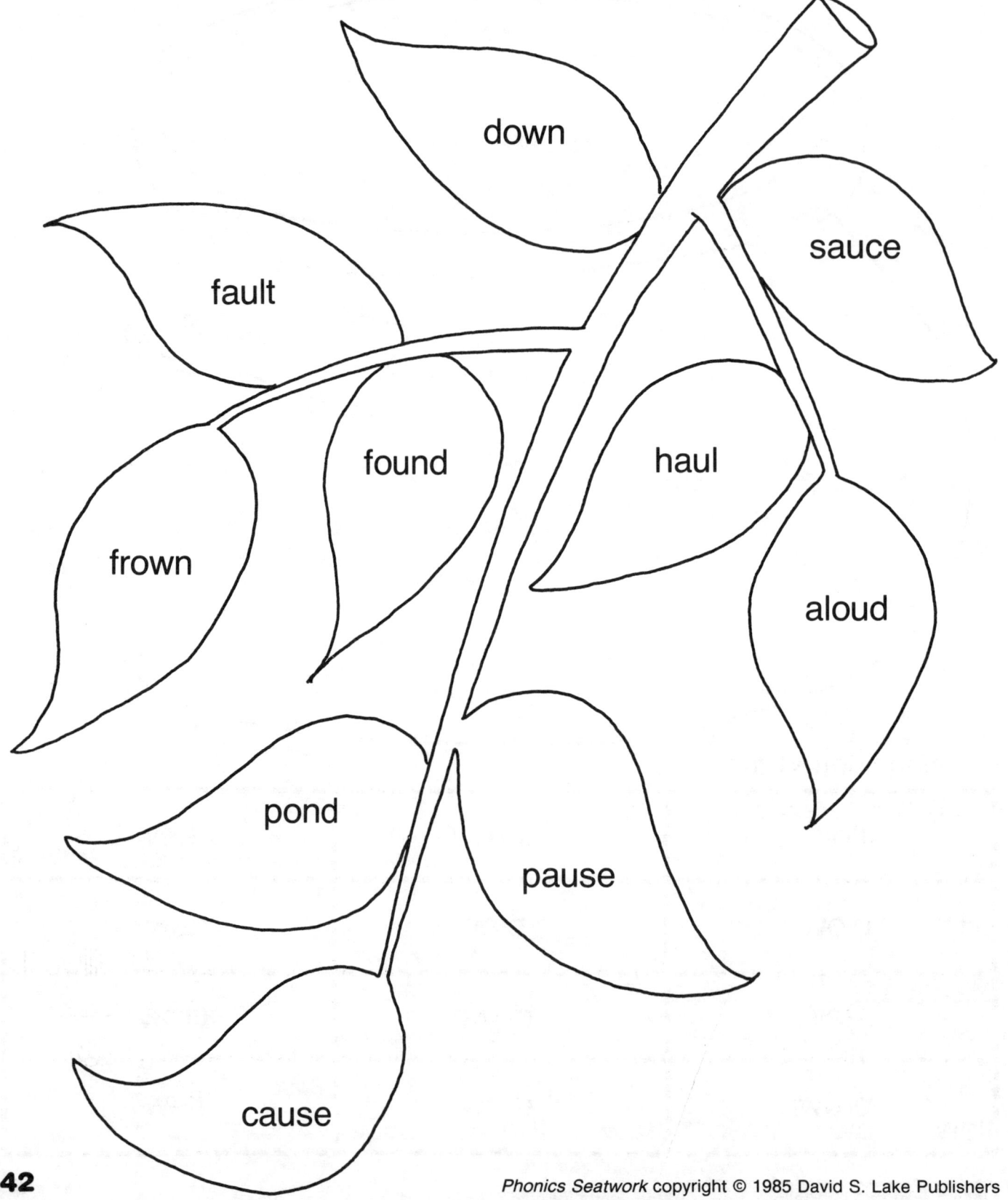

down

sauce

fault

found

haul

frown

aloud

pond

pause

cause

I Saw These Claws

Write about these claws and what they've done.
Use words with the **aw** sound as in  .

_____

- -

_____

- -

_____

- -

_____

- -

_____

            _____

            - - - - - - - - - - - - - - - - -

            _____

            - - - - - - - - - - - - -

            _____

Word List

saw	paw	straw	law	low	draw
hawk	howl	claw	awful	dawn	crawl
flow	jaw	lawn	raw	thaw	flaw

Name _____

The Garden

On the flowers and leaves in
this garden, print words with the **ar** sound as in .
Color the picture.

Word List

garden	scarf	tar	are	cart	card	care
arch	lard	hard	hare	lark	ark	mark	part
dear	arm	dart	dark	bark	jar	stare	far

What Is It?

Look at each picture. Match it with the correct word from the word list. Write the word on the line next to the picture.

1.  _____

6.  _____

2.  _____

7.  _____

3. 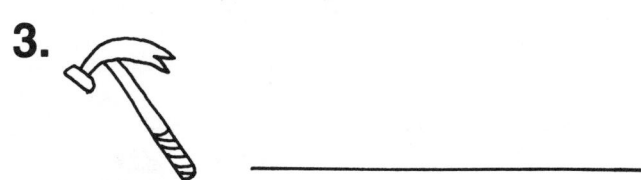 _____

8. 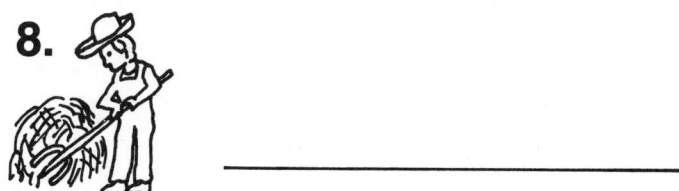 _____

4.  _____

9.  _____

5. _____

10. 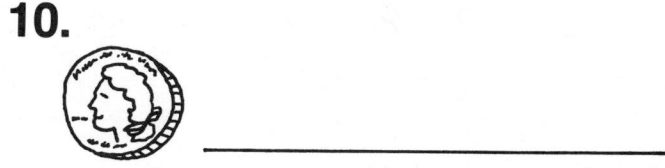 _____

Word List

feather   quarter   fern   ruler   beater   farmer

letter   pepper   lumber   hammer

Secret Code

1=A	6=F	11=K	16=P	21=U
2=B	7=G	12=L	17=Q	22=V
3=C	8=H	13=M	18=R	23=W
4=D	9=I	14=N	19=S	24=X
5=E	10=J	15=O	20=T	25=Y
				26=Z

Use the code chart to spell the words. Circle words with the **ir** sound as in 👕. Cross out the other words. The first one is done for you.

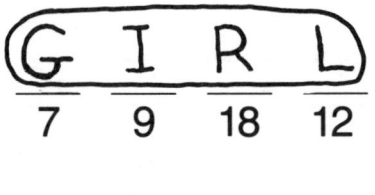

(G I R L)
7 9 18 12

3 8 9 18 16

3 9 18 3 12 5

4 9 18 20 25

6 9 18 5

19 8 9 18 20

2 9 18 20 8 4 1 25

1 4 13 9 18 5

19 20 9 18

19 11 9 18 20

6 12 9 18 20

20 9 18 5 4

A Corny Story

On the corn, print words with the **or** sound as in .
Color the picture.

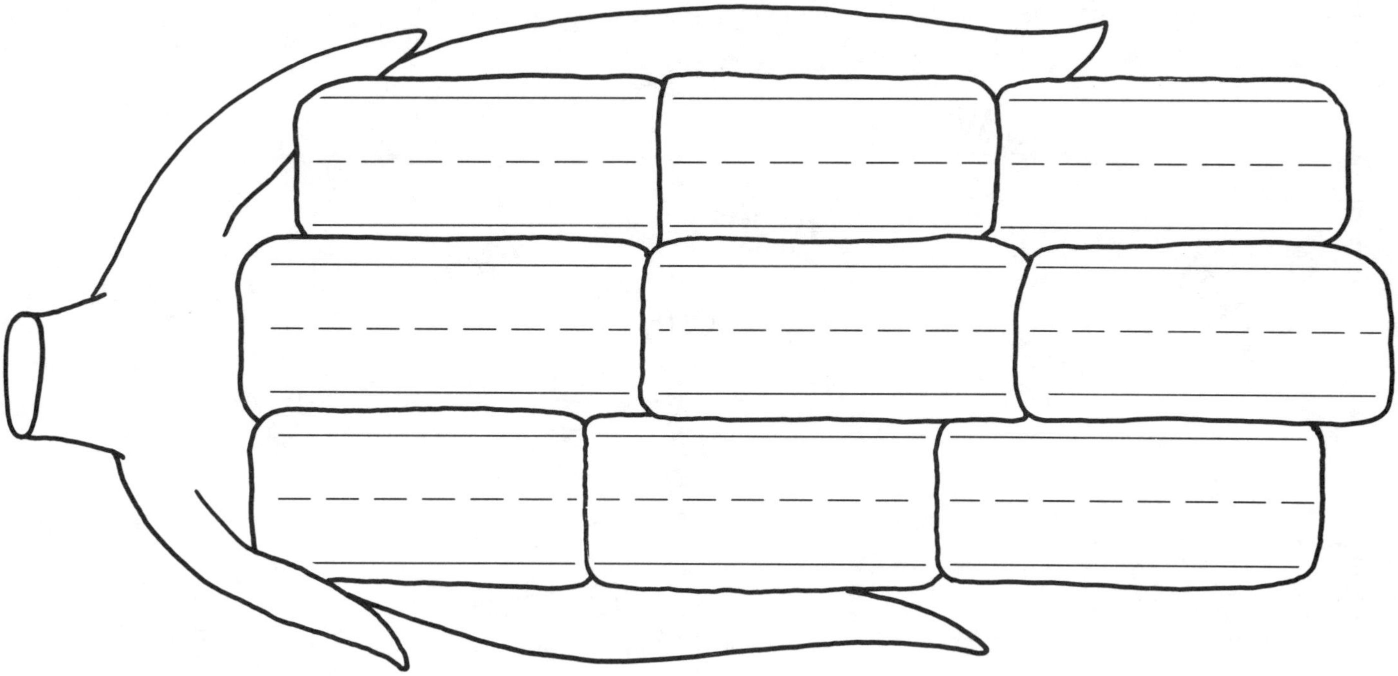

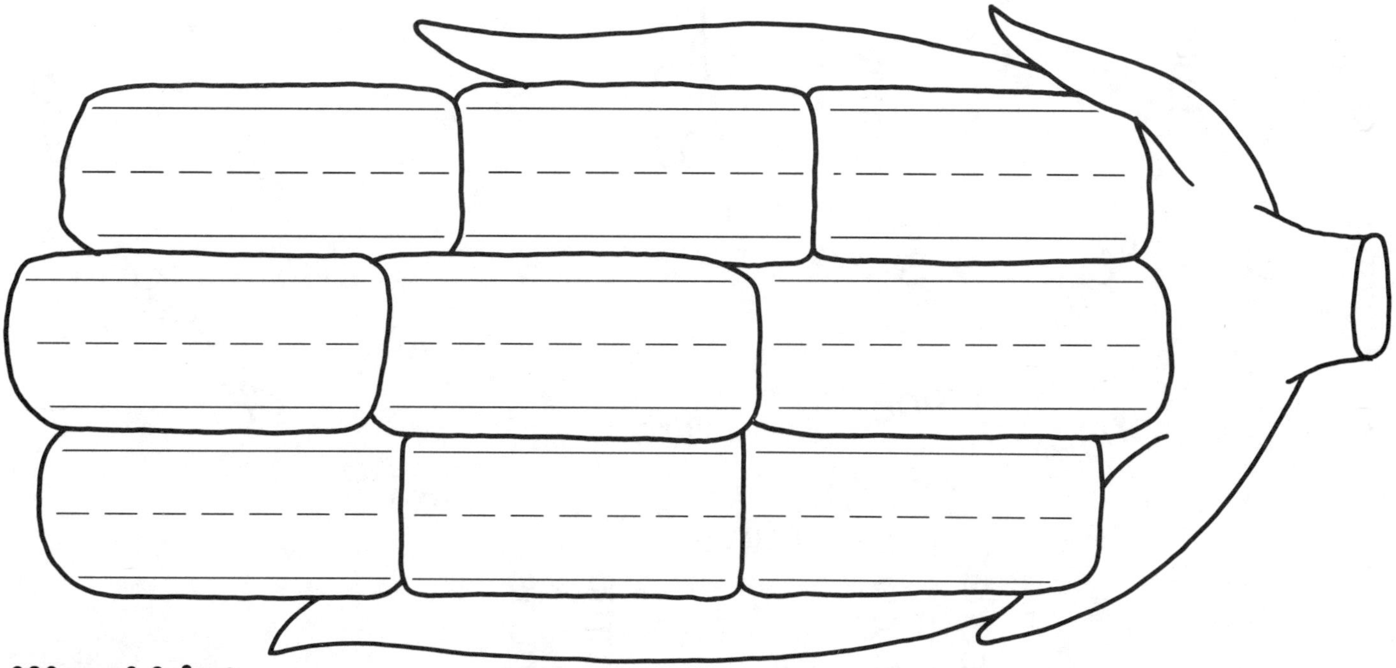

Word List

corn	sore	cork	storm	story	crow	fork
corner	short	frown	form	for	more	pork
core	store	brown	score	wore	horn	born

Phonics Seatwork copyright © 1985 David S. Lake Publishers

A Surprise Picture for You

Put a line under the words that have the **ur** sound as in 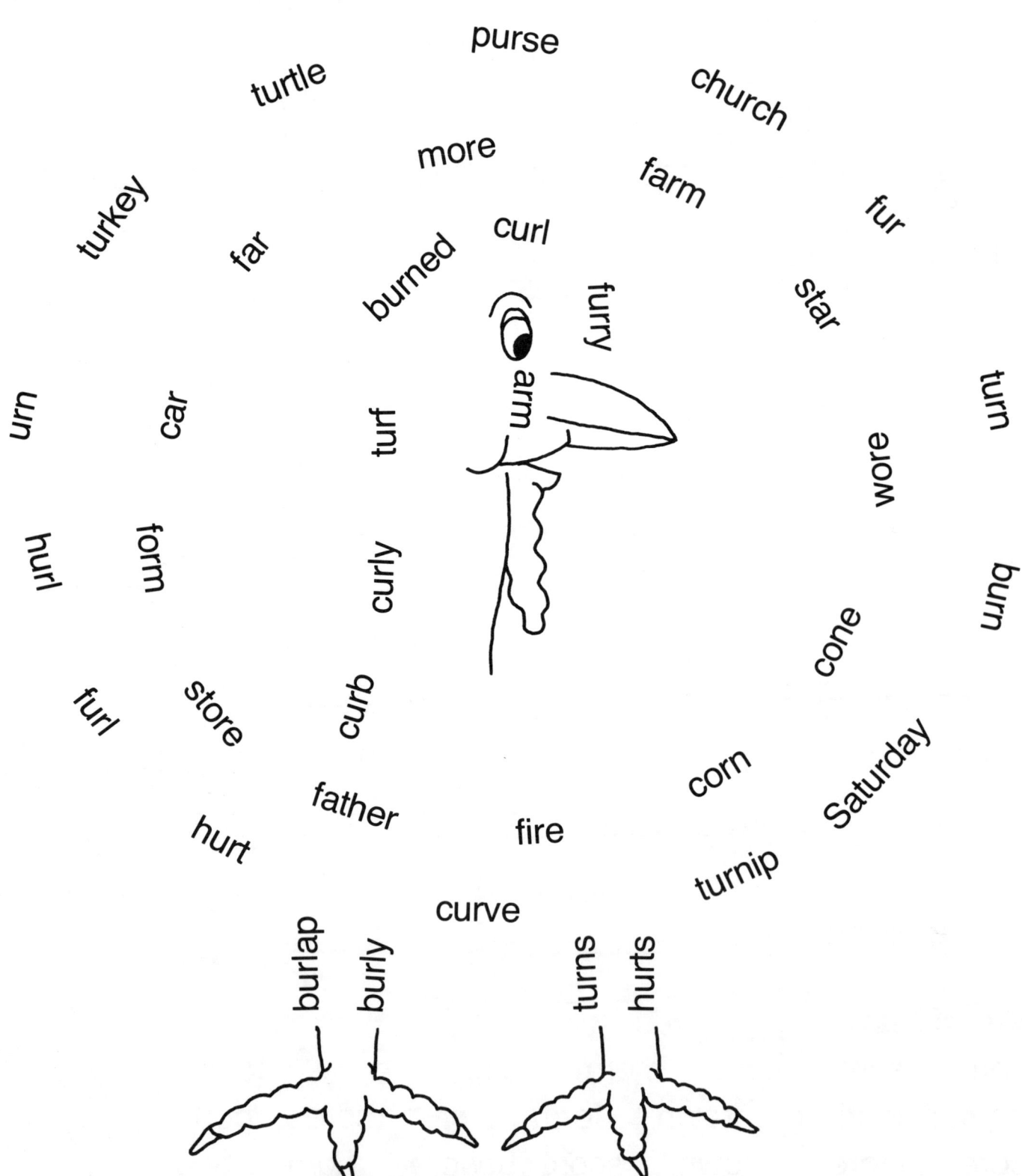.
Attach the lines to finish the drawing. Color the
picture.

purse

turtle

church

more

turkey

far

farm

fur

curl

burned

star

urn

car

turf

arm

furry

turn

wore

hurl

form

curly

cone

burn

furl

store

curb

corn

Saturday

father

fire

turnip

hurt

curve

burlap

burly

turns

hurts

Phonics Seatwork copyright © 1985 David S. Lake Publishers

Search for the Cheese

Help the mouse find the cheese. Start at **1.** Look for the words that start with the same sound as ➜🗣. Join those dots in order. Skip all the other words.

15 mostly •

1 charge •

16 cheer •

3 bold •

2 plum •

4 child •   **14** chop •   **17** change •

5 hay •   **13** baby •

6 cheap •   **12** chip •

18 check •

11 chance •

19 chairs •

7 chase •

20 call •

10 sister •

21 chocolate •   **22** banana •

8 young •

23 chin •   **25** cheese •

9 tiny •

24 chess •

Special Shoes

This boy wears only a certain kind of shoes.
Color the shoes with words
that start with the same sound as .
Draw an X through the rest.

sheep

chin

shell

shout

chip

shine

ship

chop

charge

shirt

shoe

shop

Phonics Seatwork copyright © 1985 David S. Lake Publishers

Think About This

Use the clues to choose answers from the word list. Print the answers in the correct boxes.

Across

2. Not that
3. Say "Please" and " ___ you."
4. Loud noises during a storm
5. Not these
7. When we are ___ , we drink.

Down

1. If you ___ hard, you'll get the answer.
3. The day after Wednesday
5. Not here
6. You are ___ one I love!

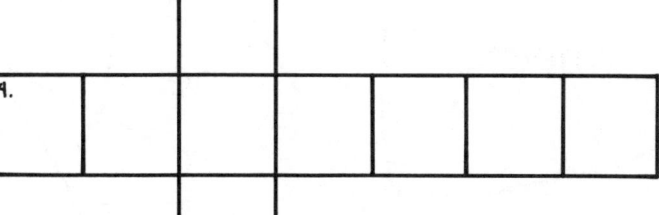

Word List

thirsty   this
there   Thursday
those   thank
think   the
thunder

What Is This Picture?

Find the words that start with the same sound as .
Color those shapes gray. Color all the other
shapes blue.

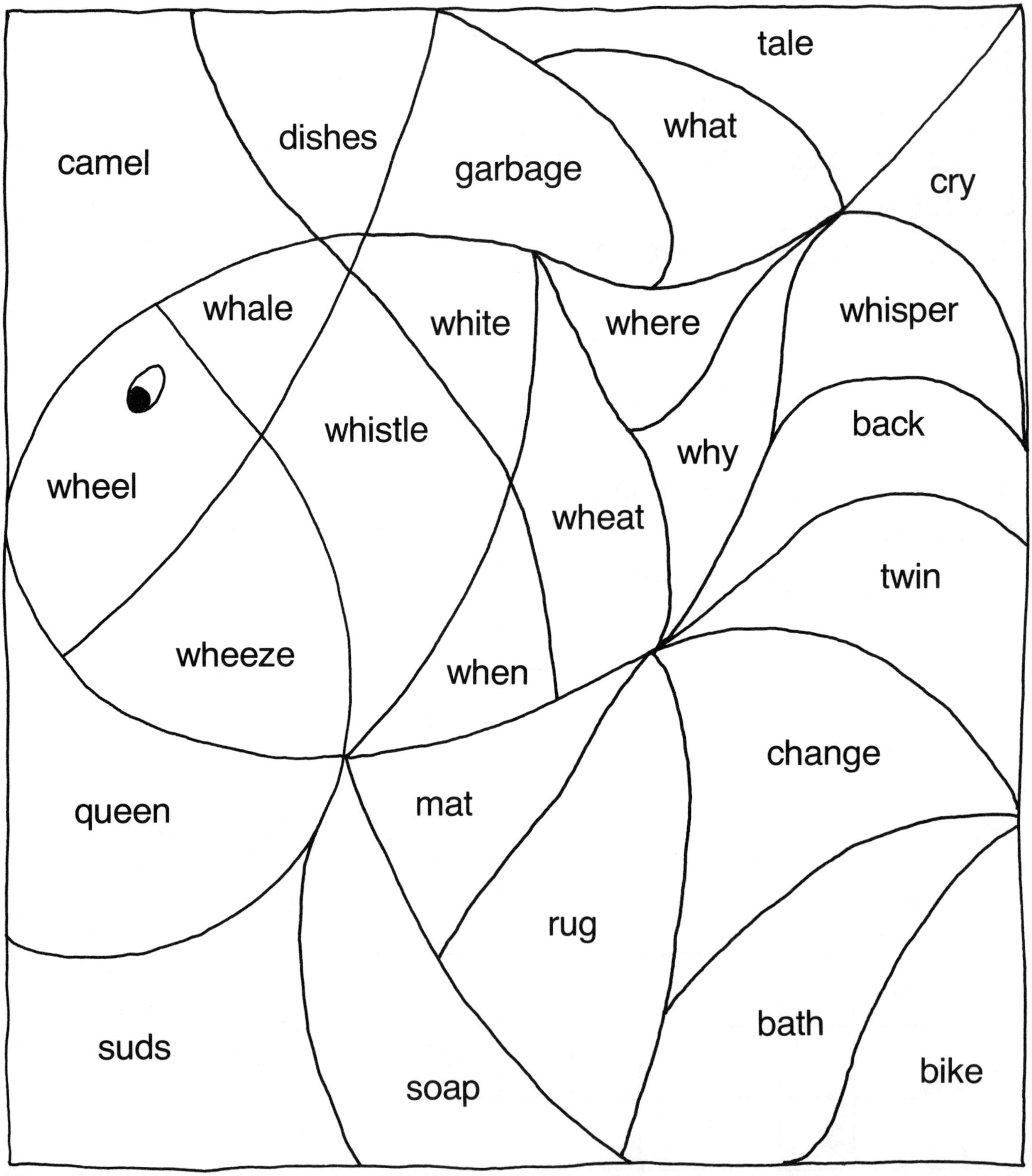

tale

dishes

what

camel

garbage

cry

whale

white

where

whisper

wheel

whistle

why

back

wheat

wheeze

when

twin

change

queen

mat

rug

suds

soap

bath

bike

Phonics Seatwork copyright © 1985 David S. Lake Publishers

Mend the Breaks

Cut out the broken pictures, and put them together. Paste the pictures on another piece of paper.

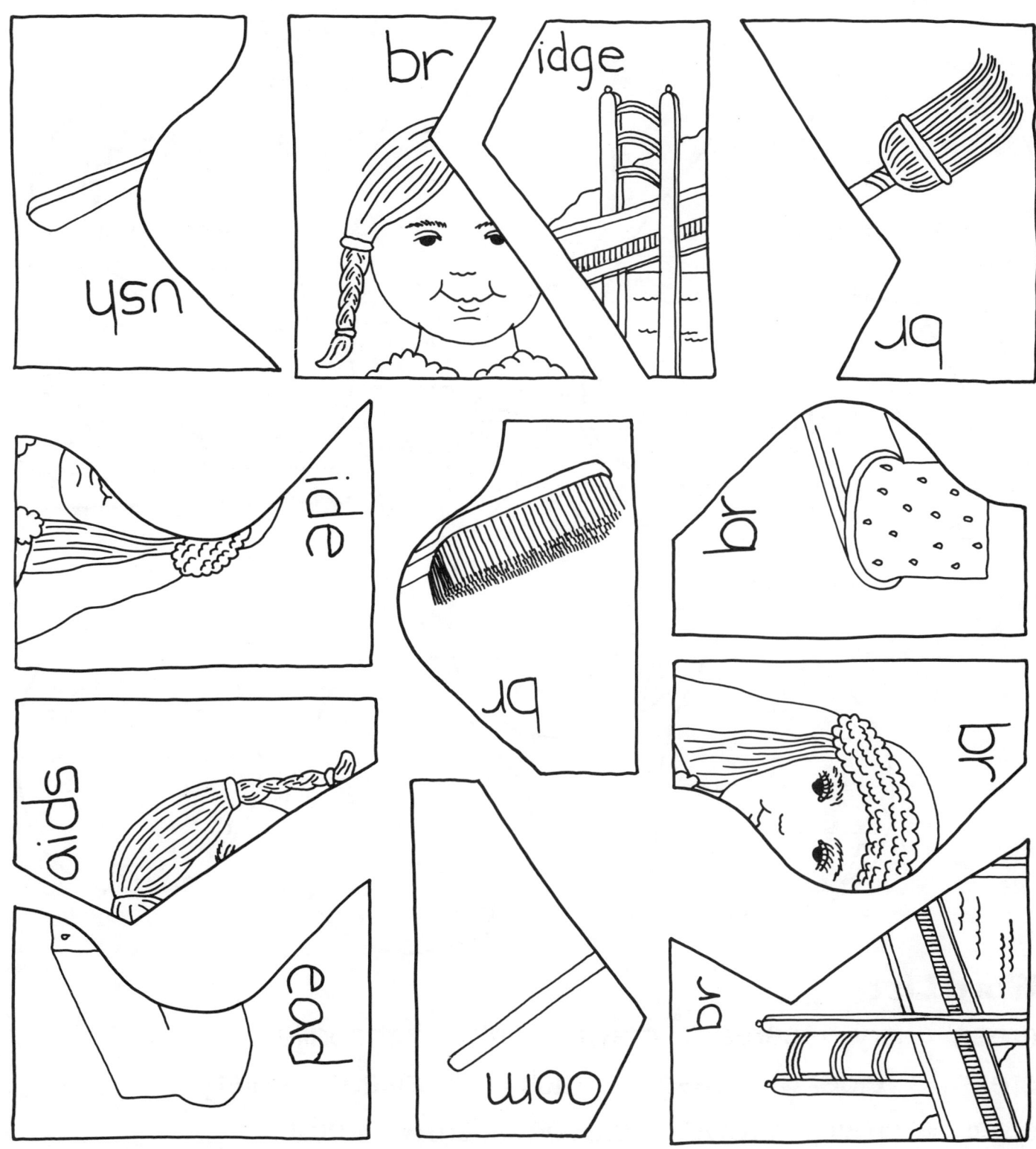

Name ______________________ **cr**

The Crying Crocodile

The crocodile is crying big crocodile tears. On the tears, print words that start with the same sound as .

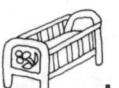

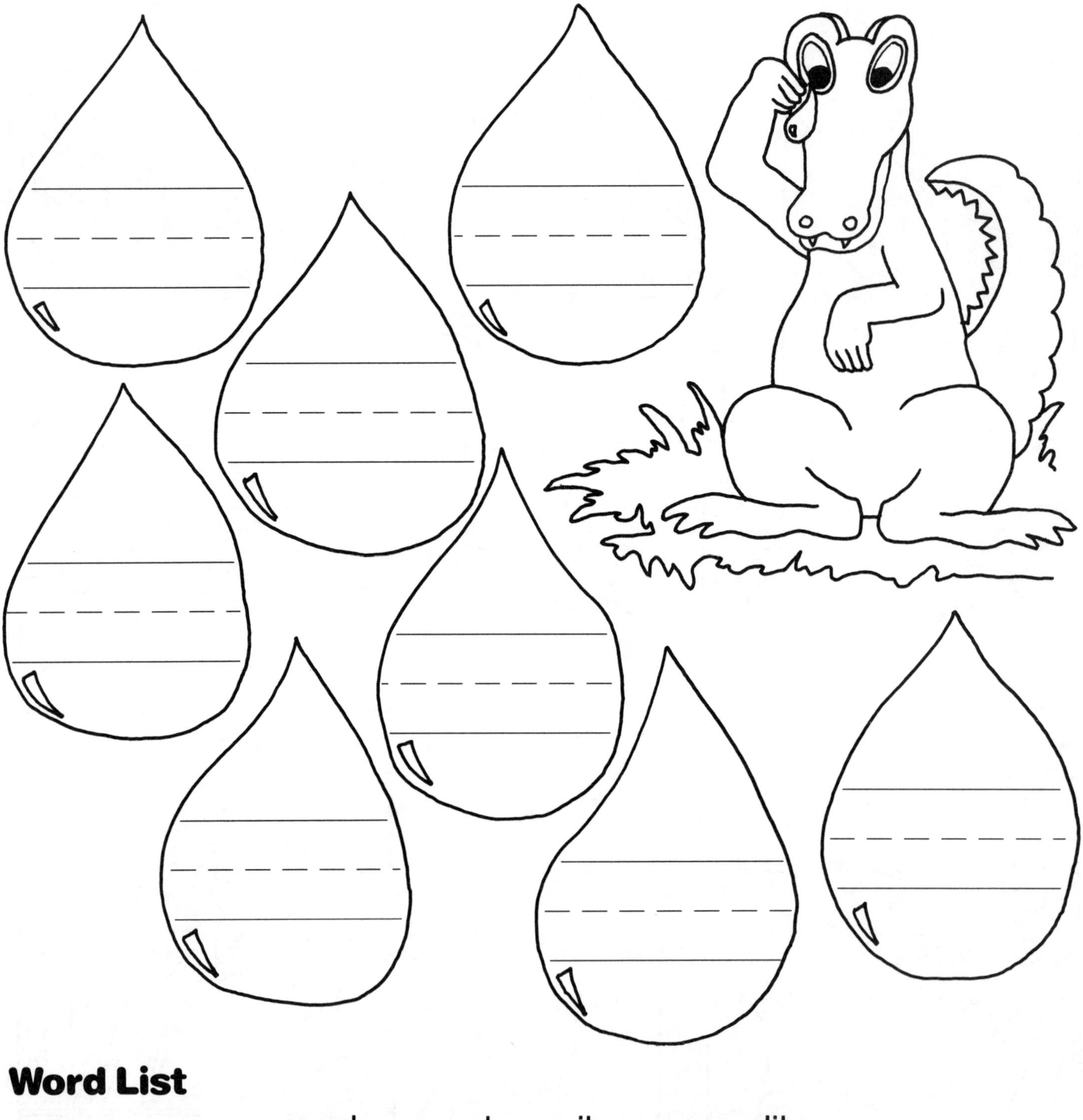

Word List

creep cry cereal crawl crib crocodile
cream cider crash crack crooked celery
cross crow crowd crayon crew cramp

Name ______________________________ **dr**

A Dry Dragon

The dragon wants a drink! Help him find the way.
Use red to color the rocks that start with the same sound as .
Color the other rocks other colors. Color the rest of the picture.

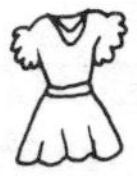

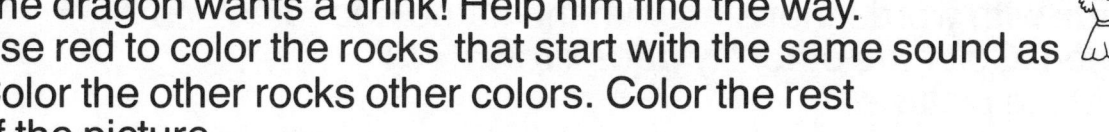

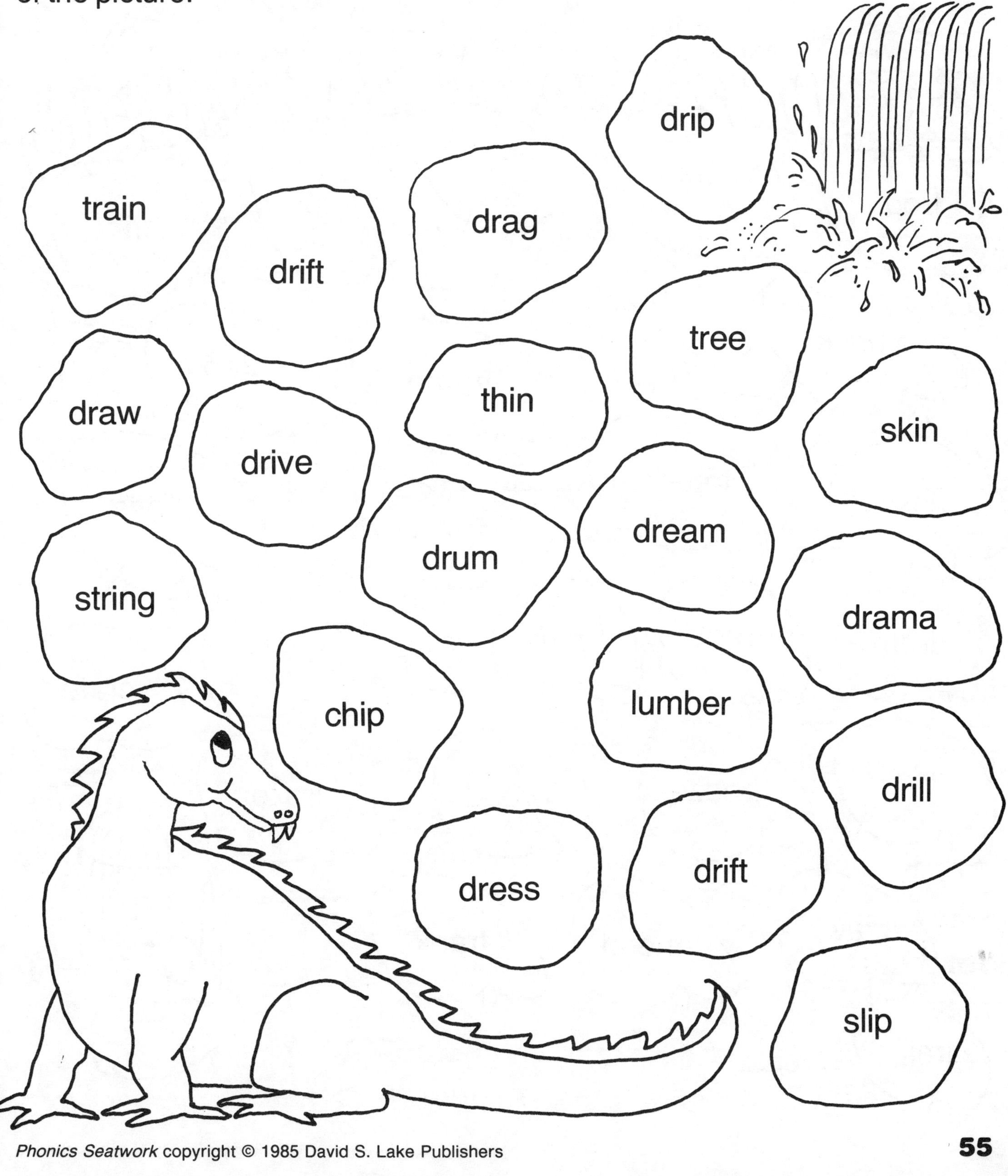

drip
train
drag
drift
tree
draw
thin
skin
drive
dream
drum
string
drama
chip
lumber
drill
dress
drift
slip

Help the Frog and His Friend

Find the lily pads with words that start with the same sound as .
Color them green. Color the other lily pads brown.
Color the rest of the picture.

frog
from
fry
fruit
crib
truck
brick
frame
crab
trick
freedom
grow
grass
drum
free
brown
cradle
crate
drip
freeze
bread
frozen
crawl
friend
frank
trail

Name _____

Trace the Trail

Circle the words that start with the same sound as 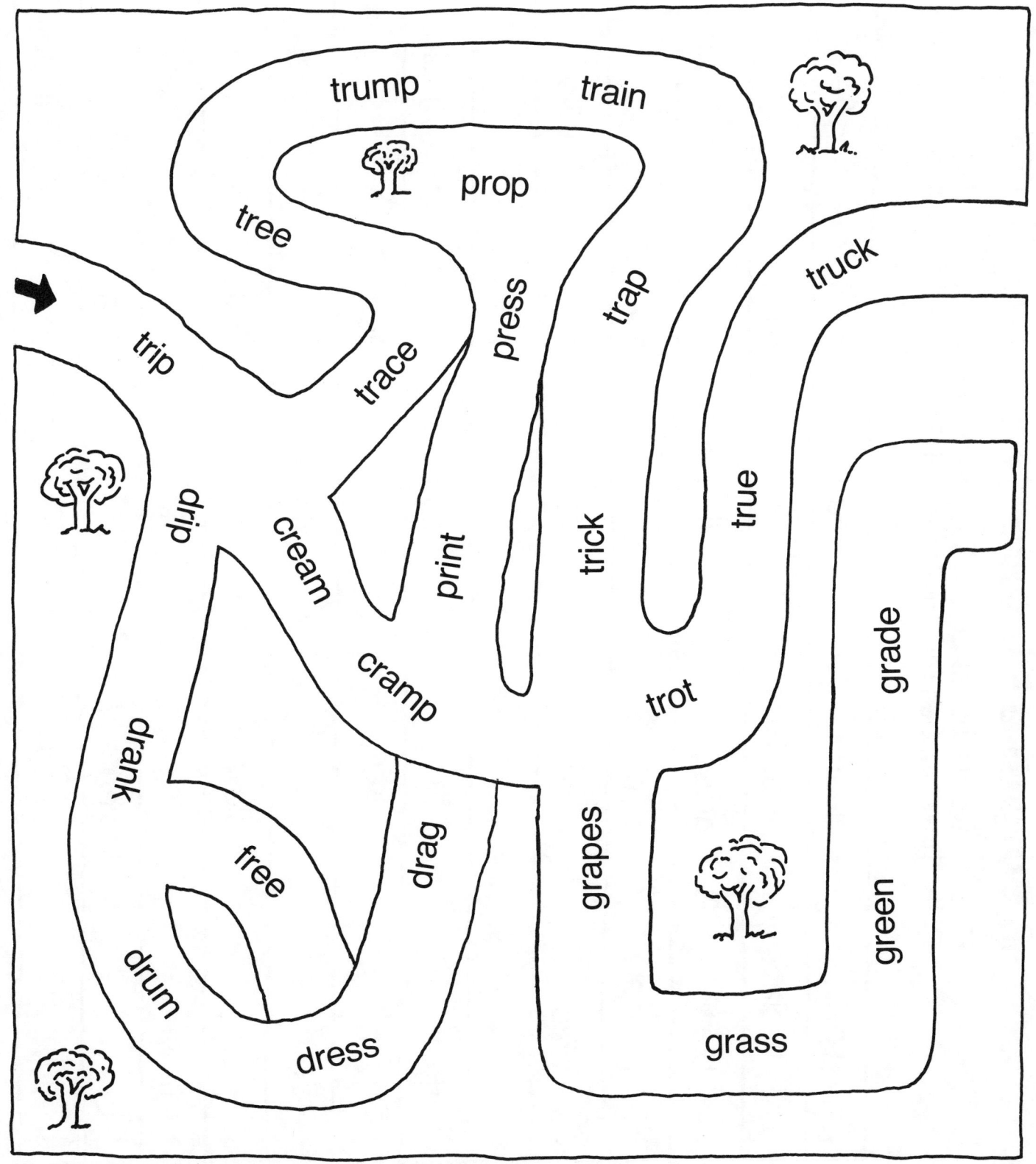.
Draw an X through the other words.

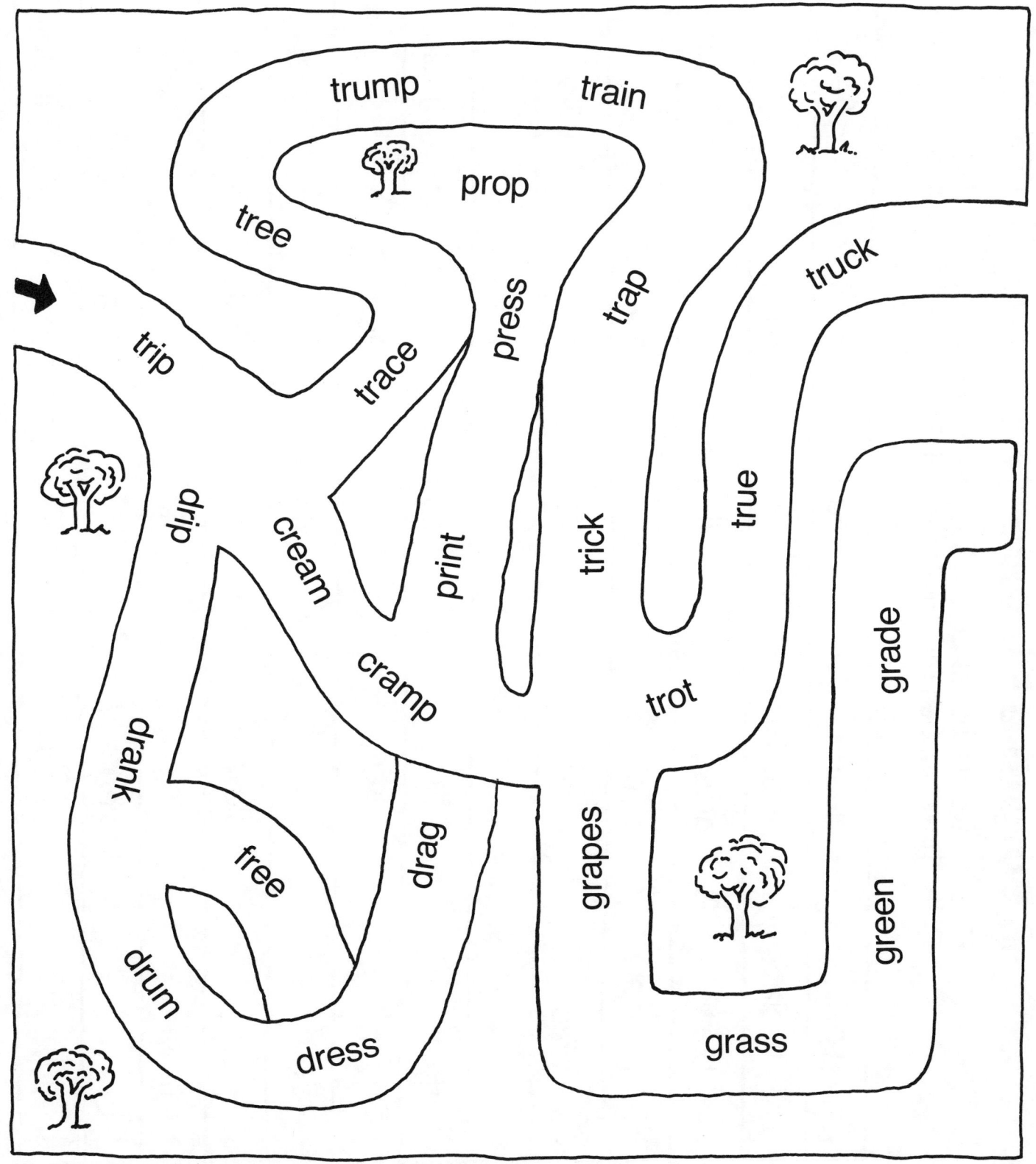

Phonics Seatwork copyright © 1985 David S. Lake Publishers

A Surprise Picture

Find the words that start with the same sound as  .
Color those shapes red. Finish the picture.

☆ glove	clean ☆	flag	clean	fled	claim
class	black			flown	blue
blew	glass	flame	slip		
claw	close	fly	play	flow	block
☆ glad	clear ☆			flock	slim
clothes		float	clue	fleet	clay
flat	blank	flood	glue	flies	plan
flavor	blame	flower			clown
flew	fling			flabby	

Spin and Spell

Cut out the small circle. Place it in the center of the big circle. Put a paper fastener through the centers of both circles. Beside the letters on the small circle, finish printing words that start with the same sound as 🕷.

Example: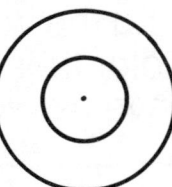

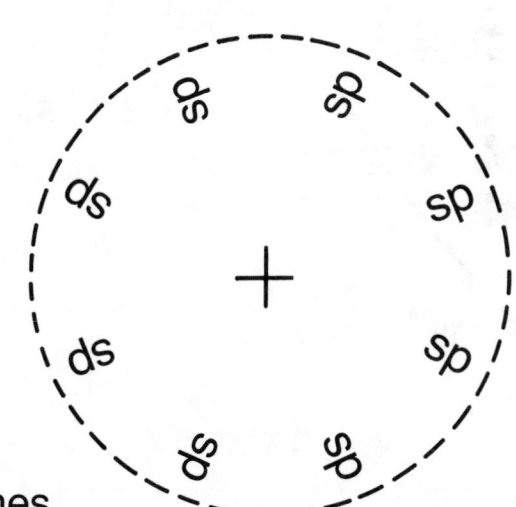

Word List

spade	spoon
soap	spill
spider	spy
spin	sip
spike	spine
spit	spoke
spell	step
sap	speed
spear	span
sport	spoil

Cut along dotted lines.

A Picture Surprise

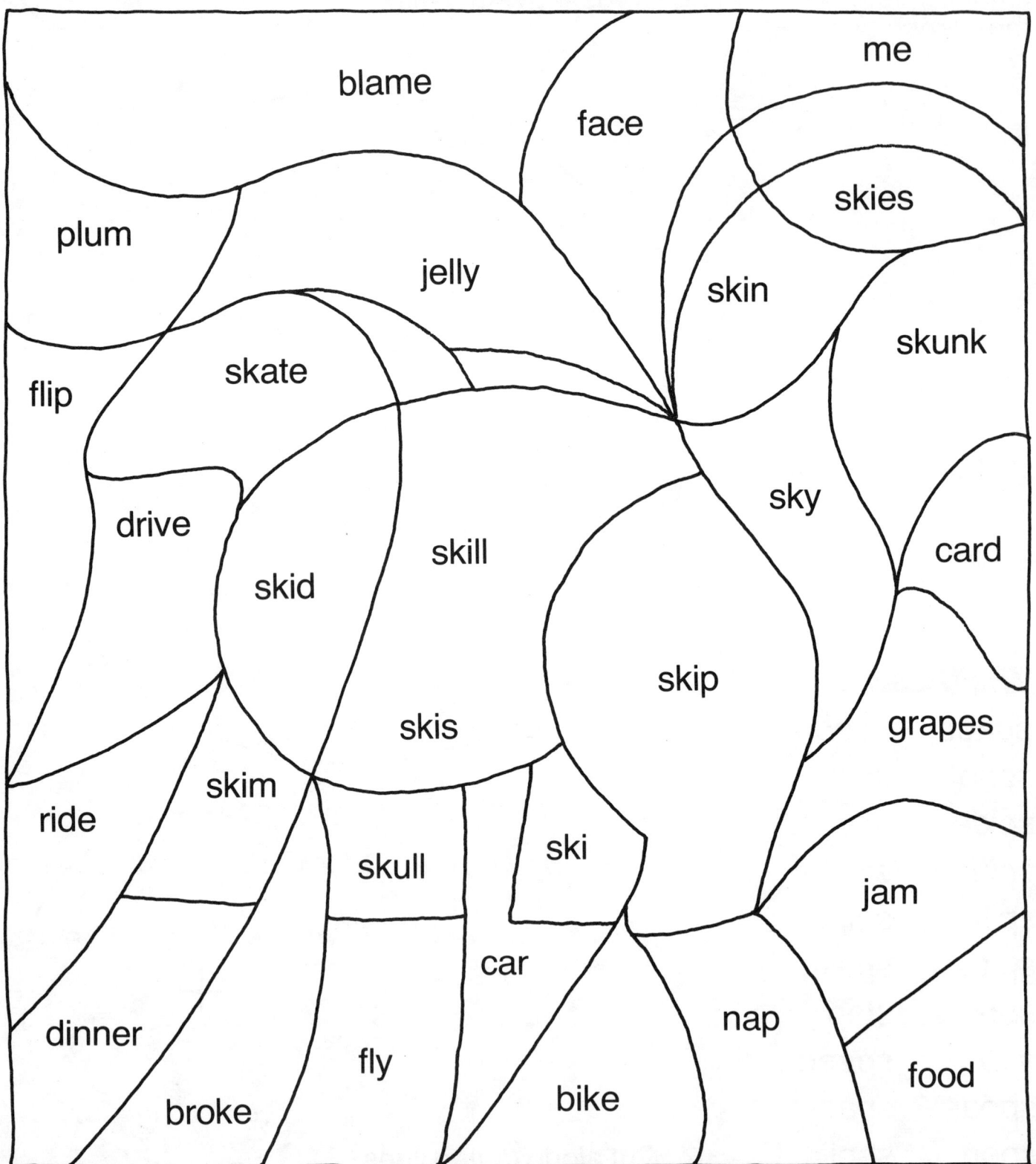

Find the words that start with the same sound as
Color those shapes black. Find the shapes that
have no words. Leave them white. Finish the picture.

blame

me

face

plum

skies

jelly

skin

skunk

skate

flip

sky

drive

skill

card

skid

skip

skis

grapes

skim

ride

ski

skull

jam

dinner

car

nap

fly

food

broke

bike

Phonics Seatwork copyright © 1985 David S. Lake Publishers